quick and easy
fitness
food

Text HELEN O'CONNOR
Styling WENDY BERECRY
Photography HARM MOL

TRIDENT PRESS
INTERNATIONAL

Introduction

What you eat can make a difference to the way you perform.
This book is packed with easy and interesting recipes that have been designed especially
to meet the needs of sportspeople. All the recipes are rated so that you can see at a
glance whether they have a high, medium or low carbohydrate, fat and fibre content.
The recipes are supported by clear and up-to-date nutrition information, all of which
helps the sportsperson to develop an eating plan to suit their individual requirements.

Published by:
TRIDENT PRESS INTERNATIONAL
801 12th Avenue South
Suite 302
Naples, FL 34102 U.S.A.
(c)Trident Press
Tel: (941) 649 7077
Fax: (941) 649 5832
Email: tridentpress@worldnet.att.net
Website: www.trident-international.com

Quick & Easy Fitness Food

EDITORIAL
Managing Editor: Rachel Blackmore
Text: Helen O'Connor BSc Dip N.D.
Food Editors: Sheryle Eastwood, Linda Venturoni
Assistant Food Editor: Anneka Mitchell
Home Economist: Donna Hay
Recipe Development: Belinda Clayton, Sue Geraghty
Editorial and Production Assistant: Heather Straton
Editorial Coordinator: Margaret Kelly

Photography: Harm Mol
Styling: Wendy Berecry

DESIGN AND PRODUCTION
Production Director: Anna Maguire
Design Manager: Drew Buckmaster
Production Coordination: Meredith Johnston
Production Editor: Sheridan Packer
Layout and Design: Lulu Dougherty

Includes Index
ISBN 1 58279 339 5
EAN 9 781582 793399

First Edition Printed August 2001

Printed by Toppan Printing, China

ABOUT THIS BOOK

NUTRITIONAL ANALYSIS
Each recipe has been computer analysed for
it kilojoule (calorie) content, carbohydrate,
fat and fibre content. The following
guidelines have been used:

CARBOHYDRATE
Rated on the percentage of energy from
carbohydrate

less than 50%	low
50-60%	medium
greater than 60%	high

FAT
Rated on the percentage of energy from fat
per serving

less than 20%	low
20-35%	medium
greater 35%	high

FIBRE

less than 2 g per serve	low
2-6 g per serve	medium
greater than 6 g per serve	high

INGREDIENTS
Unless otherwise stated the following
ingredients are used in this book:

Cream	Double, suitable for whipping
Flour	White flour, plain or standard
Sugar	White sugar

CANNED FOODS
Can sizes vary between countries and
manufacturers. You may find the quantities
in this book are slightly different to what
is available. Purchase and use the can size
nearest to the suggested size in the recipe.

MICROWAVE IT
Where microwave instructions occur in
this book, a microwave oven with an
output power of 850 watts (IEC705 –
1988) or 750 watts (AS2895 – 1986) was
used. The output power of most domestic
microwaves ranges between 600 and 900
watts (IEC705 – 1988) or 500 and 800
watts (AS2895 – 1986), so it may be
necessary to vary cooking times slightly
depending on the output power of your
microwave.

WHAT'S IN A TABLESPOON?
AUSTRALIA
1 tablespoon = 20 mL or 4 teaspoons
NEW ZEALAND
1 tablespoon = 15 mL or 3 teaspoons
UNITED KINGDOM
1 tablespoon = 15 mL or 3 teaspoons

The recipes in this book were tested in
Australia where a 20 mL tablespoon is
standard. The tablespoon in the New
Zealand and the United Kingdom sets of
measuring spoons is 15 mL. For recipes
using baking powder, gelatine, bicarbonate
of soda, small quantities of flour and
cornflour, simply add another teaspoon
for each tablespoon specified.

Contents

TACKLING THE
training diet

Regardless of the sport you play or your fitness and exercise program, the basic dietary principles are similar. The right quality and quantity of food helps active people perform at their best.

DIET CHECKLIST

Balance: A well-balanced diet is essential for good health and is the basis of peak performance.

Eat regularly: Active people in heavy training need to eat regularly to ensure that they refuel their bodies for the strenuous training sessions ahead. Nutritious snacks are also usually required to top up energy levels through the day. Those who skip meals often fail to consume adequate amounts of energy, carbohydrate, fluid and other essential nutrients.

Energy: The energy content of your diet is related to how much fuel you use each day. The more active you are, the more fuel you require. Energy needs are measured in kilojoules (calories). Balancing the energy you eat with the energy you use is essential for peak performance. Inadequate energy will result in fatigue and weight loss; excess energy will lead to weight gain.

Carbohydrate: To perform at its best the body requires the right type of fuel. No matter what your sport, carbohydrates are the best type of fuel for you. High carbohydrate diets help to enhance stamina and prevent fatigue. Complex carbohydrate (starch), which includes breakfast cereals, bread, pasta, rice and potatoes, should provide the majority of the carbohydrate eaten. Simple carbohydrate – sugar, honey, confectionery and soft drinks – should provide less than 15 per cent of your daily energy.

Fluids: The human body is 60 per cent water. During exercise some of this water is lost as sweat, and extra fluid must be consumed to replace it or dehydration occurs and the body overheats. Mild dehydration decreases athletic performance by reducing strength and stamina: severe dehydration can be life threatening. In most cases, cool water is the best fluid replacement drink.

Alcohol: While alcohol offers no benefit to athletic performance, a moderate alcohol intake is unlikely to be detrimental – providing it does not exceed 'safe limits'.

Salt: Although sweat contains salt, the amount of salt lost in training is easily replaced by a well-balanced diet – even without adding salt to food. Training also results in adaptations which improve the body's ability to conserve salt. The salt content of sweat is less in well-trained athletes. Since high-salt diets increase urine output, a 'no-added-salt' intake is recommended to ensure optimum hydration.

Protein: Sportspeople in heavy training have increased protein needs. The exact amount is still debated by experts; however 1.2-2 g of protein per kilogram of bodyweight per day is most frequently recommended. Providing the diet is well balanced and adequate for energy needs protein intake is usually not a problem. Excessive protein is not recommended, even for athletes aiming to bulk up.

Fat: Excess fat consumption has been linked with heart disease and several other modern-day diseases. Low-fat diets (diets in which less than 30 per cent of energy comes from fat) are advised for everyone, regardless of their level of activity. Fat intake can be reduced by:

- choosing lean meats and removing any visible fat;
- removing skin from poultry before cooking;
- choosing reduced-fat dairy products;
- avoiding fried foods and high-fat snacks;
- minimising the addition of fat to food – using less spreads, dressings and cooking oil. If your cholesterol is elevated, use mono-unsaturated or polyunsaturated fats and oils in place of saturated;
- invest in a nonstick frying pan and simply brush with a little oil before cooking – do not pour the oil in;
- avoid frying food – try grilling, dry-roasting on a rack, steaming, microwave cooking or wrapping in foil and baking.

Supplements: The use of vitamin and mineral supplements for athletes in heavy training remains a controversial issue and one which requires further research. To date, the majority of research has found vitamin supplements to be of no benefit to athletes who have well-balanced diets. Vitamin supplements do not compensate for a poor diet containing inadequate energy and/or carbohydrate. Supplements of iron are sometimes prescribed for athletes in heavy training who have inadequate iron stores. These supplements need to be taken under medical supervision so that iron stores can be monitored.

BLUE RIBBON
breakfasts

MIGHTY MUESLI

530 kilojoules/125 Calories per serve – high carbohydrate; medium fat; medium fibre

Oven temperature
180°C, 350°F, Gas 4

Rolled oats and coconut can be toasted in minutes in the microwave. To toast, place in separate microwavable ceramic or glass dishes and cook, separately, on HIGH (100%) until toasted. The rolled oats will take 5-6 minutes and need to be stirred every 2 minutes. The coconut will take 2-3 minutes and should be stirred every minute.

4 cups/375 g/12 oz rolled oats
2 tablespoons shredded coconut
1 cup/45 g/1¹/₂ oz oat flakes
4 tablespoons chopped dried peaches
3 tablespoons oat bran
3 tablespoons wheat germ
3 tablespoons sunflower kernels
3 tablespoons chopped dried pears
3 tablespoons currants

1 Place rolled oats and coconut in a baking dish and bake for 15-20 minutes or until toasted. Stir several times during cooking to ensure even toasting. Cool.

2 Place rolled oats mixture, oat flakes, peaches, oat bran, wheat germ, sunflower kernels, pears and currants in a bowl and mix to combine.

Serving suggestion: Sprinkle with banana chips and top with icy cold low-fat milk or juice.

Makes 20 servings

BANANA YOGURT TOPPING

120 kilojoules/30 Calories per serve – high carbohydrate; low fat; low fibre

1 banana, sliced
³/₄ cup/155 g/5 oz low-fat
natural yogurt
¹/₂ teaspoon ground cinnamon

Place banana, yogurt and cinnamon in a bowl and mix to combine.

Serving suggestion: Use as a topping for pancakes, or spoon over cereal or fruit.

Makes 1 cup/250 g/8 oz

Spring Omelette, Berry Sauce (recipes pages 10);
Spicy Buckwheat Pancakes (page 10)
with Banana Yogurt Topping, Mighty Muesli

SPICY BUCKWHEAT PANCAKES

565 kilojoules/135 Calories per serve – high carbohydrate; low fat; low fibre

¼ cup/30 g/1 oz buckwheat flour
¼ cup/30 g/1 oz self-raising flour
1 teaspoon ground allspice
1 cup/250 mL/8 fl oz skim milk
1 tablespoon honey, warmed
1 egg white, lightly beaten
1 teaspoon vegetable oil
1 teaspoon grated lemon rind

1 Sift buckwheat and self-raising flours and allspice together into a bowl. Combine milk, honey, egg white and oil. Add to flour mixture and mix to make a smooth batter. Stir in lemon rind.

2 Drop tablespoons of mixture into a heated nonstick frying pan and cook until golden on both sides.

Serves 4

Serve pancakes topped with Banana Yogurt Topping (page 8) or Berry Sauce (this page). They are also delicious served plain.

BERRY SAUCE

55 kilojoules/15 Calories per serve – high carbohydrate; low fat; low fibre

250 g/8 oz mixed berries, fresh or frozen
2 tablespoons apple juice

Place berries in a food processor or blender and process until smooth. Push through a sieve to remove seeds, then stir in apple juice.

Makes 1 cup/250 mL/8 fl oz

Delicious served over pancakes, cereal or fruit.

SPRING OMELETTE

570 kilojoules/135 Calories per serve – low carbohydrate; high fat; low fibre

4 eggs, lightly beaten
¼ cup/60 mL/2 fl oz skim milk
freshly ground black pepper
1 teaspoon polyunsaturated margarine
3 tablespoons grated reduced-fat cheddar cheese

VEGETABLE FILLING
1 teaspoon polyunsaturated margarine
6 button mushrooms, sliced
½ small red pepper, sliced
2 spring onions, finely chopped
1 teaspoon chopped fresh coriander

1 To make filling, melt margarine in a nonstick frying pan over a medium heat, add mushrooms, red pepper, spring onions and coriander and cook, stirring for 2 minutes or until vegetables are tender. Remove from pan and keep warm.

2 Place eggs, milk and black pepper to taste in a bowl and whisk to combine. Melt remaining margarine in a clean nonstick frying pan over a medium heat. Pour egg mixture into pan and cook until almost set. Place filling on one half of the omelette, then sprinkle with cheese. Fold omelette over, cut in half, slide onto serving plates and serve immediately.

Start your breakfast with fresh fruit then serve the omelette with crisp toast.

Serves 2

*Fruit and Nut Muffins (page 12),
Peaches and Cream Muffins,
Three T Muffins*

PEACHES AND CREAM MUFFINS

950 kilojoules/225 Calories per serve – high carbohydrate; low fat; medium fibre

¹/₃ cup/90 g/3 oz low-fat cottage
cheese
pulp of 1 passion fruit
2 muffins, halved and toasted
2 peaches, stoned and sliced

Combine cottage cheese and passion
fruit pulp. Spread mixture over muffins,
top with peach slices and serve.

Serves 2

THREE T MUFFINS

1055 kilojoules/250 Calories per serve – medium carbohydrate; low fat; medium fibre

1 tomato, sliced
2 muffins, halved and toasted
2 slices cooked turkey breast
3 tablespoons grated low-fat
cheddar cheese
freshly ground black pepper

Place tomato slices on muffins. Top
with turkey, cheese and black pepper to
taste. Place under a preheated hot grill
and cook until heated through.

Serves 2

Use wholemeal or mixed
grain muffins to increase
fibre intake.

11

VEGETABLE HASH BROWNS

500 kilojoules/120 Calories per serve – low carbohydrate; high fat; medium fibre

2 potatoes, grated
1 carrot, grated
1 zucchini, grated
1 tablespoon poppy seeds
2 eggs, lightly beaten
freshly ground black pepper
1 tablespoon polyunsaturated
vegetable oil

1 Place potatoes, carrot, zucchini, poppy seeds, eggs and black pepper to taste in a bowl and mix to combine.

2 Lightly brush or spray a nonstick frying pan with oil and heat over a medium heat. Place spoonfuls of mixture in pan, flatten slightly and cook for 4-5 minutes each side or until golden.

Serving suggestion: For a complete breakfast, start with a glass of skim milk and fresh fruit and serve hash browns with bread or toast.

Serves 4

As an alternative to skim milk, serve with one of the drinks from Dive into a Drink (see page 48).

FRUIT AND NUT MUFFINS

1240 kilojoules/295 Calories per serve – medium carbohydrate; medium fat; medium fibre

^{1}/₃ cup/90 g/3 oz reduced-fat ricotta cheese
1 tablespoon currants
1 tablespoon chopped raisins
1 teaspoon grated orange rind
2 muffins, halved and toasted
2 tablespoons chopped pecans

Combine ricotta cheese, currants, raisins and orange rind. Spread mixture over muffins, sprinkle with pecans and serve.

Serves 2

CARBOHYDRATE CHARGES
Top ready-made cereals with any of the following to add extra energy, fibre or carbohydrate:
•   dried fruit, such as figs, sultanas, raisins, apricots or dates
•   mashed or sliced bananas
•   stewed or canned fruits, such as apples, pears, peaches or pineapples
•   a drizzle of honey or a sprinkle of sugar
•   chopped nuts
•   a sprinkle of sesame, sunflower or pumpkin seeds
•   a spoonful of wheat germ, lecithin or bran
•   low-fat yogurt for extra calcium
•   fortified milk for extra calcium, protein and energy

FRUITY PORRIDGE POWER

2050 kilojoules/490 Calories per serve – high carbohydrate; low fat; low fibre

1 small apple, cored and chopped
3 tablespoons chopped dried apricots
^{1}/₂ cup/125 mL/4 fl oz water
2 cups/500 mL/16 fl oz skim milk
1^1/₂ cups/140 g/4^1/₂ oz instant rolled oats
2 tablespoons sultanas
1 teaspoon ground mixed spice

1 Place apple, apricots and water in a saucepan and bring to the boil. Reduce heat and simmer for 5 minutes or until fruit is tender.

2 Place milk in a separate saucepan and heat gently for 2-3 minutes. Stir in rolled oats and bring to the boil. Cook, stirring constantly, for 1 minute. Stir in sultanas, mixed spice and apple mixture.

Serving suggestion: Top with extra skim milk and sprinkle with grated nutmeg.

Serves 2

TASTY HAWAIIAN POCKETS

1415 kilojoules/335 Calories per serve - high carbohydrate; low fat; medium fibre

4 small wholemeal pocket breads

HAWAIIAN FILLING
220 g/7 oz canned pineapple pieces, drained and chopped
½ cup/125 g/4 oz low-fat cottage cheese
4 slices reduced-fat-and-salt ham, finely chopped
3 tablespoons grated low-fat cheddar cheese
1 tablespoon snipped fresh chives
freshly ground black pepper
1 teaspoon polyunsaturated vegetable oil

1 To make filling, place pineapple, cottage cheese, ham, cheddar cheese, chives and black pepper to taste in a bowl and mix to combine.

2 Make a small slit in the side of each pocket bread and spoon in filling. Brush a nonstick frying pan with oil and heat over a medium heat. Cook pockets for 3 minutes each side or until crisp and heated through.

Serving suggestion: Accompany with a fruit smoothie (see page 48).

Serves 4

Oven temperature
180°C, 350°F, Gas 4

The unsweetened varieties of canned fruits and juices will cut kilojoules (calories) without affecting the recipe, so are a good alternative for those watching their weight.

Vegetable Hash Browns, Fruity Porridge Power, Tasty Hawaiian Pockets

LUNCH
on the run

GOLDEN GRAIN SALAD

2590 kilojoules/620 Calories per serve – high carbohydrate; low fat; high fibre

1 cup/220 g/7 oz brown rice, cooked
1 cup/220 g/7 oz pearl barley, cooked
$^1/_3$ cup/60 g/2 oz couscous, cooked
440 g/14 oz canned no-added-salt
    sweet corn kernels, drained
1 green pepper, cut into strips
1 carrot, peeled and cut into strips
1 zucchini (courgette), cut into strips
2 stalks celery, cut into strips

ORANGE DRESSING
2 teaspoons wholegrain mustard
1 teaspoon grated fresh ginger
$^1/_2$ cup/125 mL/4 fl oz orange juice
freshly ground black pepper

1 Place rice, barley, couscous, sweet corn, green pepper, carrot, zucchini (courgette) and celery in a bowl.

2 To make dressing, place mustard, ginger, orange juice and black pepper to taste in a screwtop jar and shake to combine. Pour over salad and toss.

Serves 4

Keep a selection of cooked rice, pasta and legumes in the refrigerator then you will always have a carbohydrate-rich food that can be made into a salad in minutes. Always cook extra of these foods to have on hand.

CHICKEN PASTA ROLLS

1200 kilojoules/285 Calories per serve – low carbohydrate; medium fat; medium fibre

12 spinach or wholemeal lasagne sheets
2 tablespoons grated parmesan cheese

CHICKEN AND LEEK FILLING
2 teaspoons polyunsaturated
    vegetable oil
3 chicken breast fillets, cut into strips
3 leeks, finely sliced
2 tablespoons chopped fresh basil
1 teaspoon French mustard
$^1/_2$ cup/125 mL/4 fl oz chicken stock
3 teaspoons cornflour blended with
    2 tablespoons of water

1 Cook lasagne sheets in boiling water in a saucepan until tender. Drain and keep warm.

2 To make filling, heat oil in a frying pan over a medium heat, add chicken and leeks and cook for 4-5 minutes or until brown. Stir in basil, mustard, stock and cornflour mixture and cook, stirring, for 2 minutes.

3 Place spoonfuls of filling on lasagne sheets and roll up. Sprinkle with parmesan cheese and serve immediately.

Serving suggestion: For extra fibre and carbohydrate serve with a green salad and crusty wholemeal bread.

Serves 4

Lunch should include a variety of foods and supply about one-third of your daily nutrient needs.

Multi-layered Bread Loaf (page 16), Golden Grain Salad, Chicken Pasta Rolls

14

Multi-layered Bread Loaf

2965 kilojoules/710 Calories per serve – high carbohydrate; low fat; high fibre

1 small round rye cottage loaf
2 tablespoons reduced-fat mayonnaise
1 tablespoon wholegrain mustard
4 cos lettuce leaves
4 mignonette lettuce leaves
15 g/¹/₂ oz alfalfa sprouts
125 g/4 oz canned no-added-salt
pink salmon, drained
2 spring onions, finely chopped
30 g/1 oz snow pea (mangetout)
sprouts or watercress
2 tomatoes, sliced
¹/₂ cucumber, sliced
1 tablespoon chopped fresh basil
freshly ground black pepper

Serves 2

1 Cut bread horizontally into four even layers. Combine mayonnaise and mustard and spread over each bread layer.

2 Arrange cos and mignonette lettuce leaves and sprouts over bottom bread layer. Top with next bread layer. Then spread with salmon and top with spring onions and snow pea (mangetout) sprouts or watercress. Top with next bread layer, then arrange tomato and cucumber slices over bread, sprinkle with basil and black pepper to taste. Finally top with remaining bread round.

Serving suggestion: Cut into wedges and accompany with fresh fruit.

This multi-layered sandwich could also be made using individual bread rolls. Choose two large bread rolls in place of the cottage loaf. Cut each roll horizontally into four even layers and assemble as described in recipe, remembering to divide the ingredients evenly between each roll.

Health Club Sandwiches

1895 kilojoules/450 Calories per serve – medium carbohydrate; medium fat; high fibre

1 tablespoon 'lite' margarine
4 slices rye bread
4 slices wholegrain bread
1 curly endive
4 slices reduced-fat-and-salt ham
2 tomatoes, sliced
4 slices pumpernickel bread
4 slices reduced-fat cheddar cheese
¹/₂ bunch watercress

1 Spread margarine thinly on one side of each slice of rye and wholegrain bread. Top rye bread with endive leaves, ham and tomato slices, then with slices of pumpernickel bread.

2 Place cheese and watercress on pumpernickel bread and top with wholegrain bread. Cut each sandwich in half and serve immediately.

Serves 4

Preparing lunch for school or work the night before will help avoid the morning rush.

Super 'Sand-wedges'

Sandwiches remain the most popular and convenient lunch for people 'on the go'. Changing the type of bread and filling helps to prevent boredom. Try some of the following ideas and remember to use as little margarine or butter as possible – better still, leave it off altogether.

SERVING SUGGESTIONS

Tri-wedges: Include a third piece of bread in the centre of the sandwich – it adds extra carbohydrate.

Toast-wedges: When you feel like something hot, toast your sandwich under a grill, or cook it in a sandwich maker. Preheat the grill or sandwich maker while making the sandwich.

Pocket-wedges: Place filling in a pocket bread.

Roll-wedges: Place fillings on pitta bread and roll up. One large round is equivalent to four slices of bread.

Continental-wedges: Try some of the different breads and rolls – check out the supermarket and local bakery.

Crisp-wedges: Top crispbread or rice cakes with fillings of your choice.

FILLING IDEAS

• Lean roast meat with pickle, mustard or chutney and lettuce, tomato or salad.

• Skinless cooked chicken or turkey with cranberry sauce or reduced-fat mayonnaise and lettuce, celery, avocado, celery, sprouts or nuts.

• Reduced-fat cheese with celery, lettuce, grated carrot and sultanas, canned or fresh pineapple slices or gherkin.

• Low-fat cottage or reduced-fat ricotta cheese with dried fruit, chopped walnuts, pine nuts, lettuce, salad, tomato, grated carrot and sultanas, chopped dried dates, wholegrain mustard, hummus or tahini.

• Canned tuna, salmon or sardines with lettuce, celery, spring onions, sprouts, tomato, gherkin, grated carrot or cucumber and reduced-fat mayonnaise.

• Peanut butter (try no-added-salt) with banana, honey, carrot and alfalfa, or low-fat cottage cheese and raisins.

• Sweet corn with reduced-fat-and-salt ham and lettuce, or grated reduced-fat cheese, or chives and radish.

• Baked beans or bean mixes with lettuce and grated reduced-fat cheese or sliced onion and mushroom.

TURBO TOPPERS

Bread, muffins and crumpets topped with favourite foods are quick and easy and add extra carbohydrate and energy. For quick topping ideas try the following:

• spaghetti, baked beans or sweet corn kernels – use the no-added-salt varieties

• low-fat cottage cheese with raisins and nuts

• mashed bananas and cinnamon

• low-fat cottage cheese and fruit chutney

• peanut butter and honey

• grilled fresh or canned pineapple and cheese

• mashed pumpkin and cracked black pepper

Health Club Sandwiches

VEGETABLE AND SALAD ROLL-UPS

855 kilojoules/205 Calories per serve – medium carbohydrate; low fat; high fibre

4 wholemeal Lebanese or
pitta bread rounds
4 tablespoons reduced-fat mayonnaise
8 lettuce leaves, shredded
2 tomatoes, sliced
1 beetroot, peeled and grated

SOYA PATTIES
440 g/14 oz canned soya beans,
rinsed, drained and roughly mashed
1 cup/60 g/2 oz wholemeal
breadcrumbs, made from stale bread
1 carrot, grated
1 zucchini (courgette), grated
1/2 teaspoon ground cumin
2 tablespoons no-added-salted
tomato paste (purée)
1 egg white

1 To make patties, place soya beans, breadcrumbs, carrot, zucchini (courgette), cumin, tomato paste (purée) and egg white in a bowl and mix to combine. Shape mixture into 12 small patties and cook in a nonstick frying pan over a medium heat for 3 minutes each side or until golden. Keep warm.

2 Spread bread rounds with mayonnaise. Divide lettuce leaves, tomato slices, beetroot and patties evenly between bread rounds. Roll up to form a cylinder and serve immediately.

Serves 4

To keep summer lunches cool, pack frozen fruit pieces or fruit drinks in the container next to the salads and sandwiches.

TORTELLINI SALAD

1860 kilojoules/445 Calories per serve – high carbohydrate; low fat; high fibre

750 g/1 1/2 lb mixed-coloured
veal tortellini
250 g/8 oz asparagus, cut into
5 cm/2 in pieces
185 g/6 oz snow peas (mangetout)
1 butter lettuce
1 red pepper, sliced
250 g/8 oz yellow cherry tomatoes
1/2 cup/125 mL/4 fl oz no-oil Italian
dressing

1 Cook tortellini in boiling water in a large saucepan, following packet directions. Drain, rinse under cold water and cool.

2 Boil, steam or microwave asparagus and snow peas (mangetout), separately, until tender. Refresh under cold running water and set aside.

3 Arrange lettuce, red pepper, tomatoes, tortellini, asparagus and snow peas (mangetout) in bowl or on a platter. Drizzle with dressing and serve immediately.

Serves 4

Cook the pasta and vegetables for this salad in advance and store in the refrigerator for up to 2 days. The salad only takes minutes to assemble.

*Tortellini Salad; Tri-potato Salad,
Herb and Chicken Burgers (recipes page 20),
Vegetable and Salad Roll-ups*

HERB AND CHICKEN BURGERS

2140 kilojoules/510 Calories per serve – low carbohydrate; medium fat; high fibre

4 boneless chicken breast fillets, approximately 125 g/4 oz each
4 round, wholegrain bread rolls, halved and toasted
12 cherry tomatoes, sliced
1 curly endive

HERB MAYONNAISE
2 teaspoons snipped fresh chives
2 teaspoons chopped fresh parsley
4 tablespoons reduced-fat mayonnaise

1 To make Herb Mayonnaise, place chives, parsley and mayonnaise in a bowl and mix to combine.

2 Heat a nonstick frying pan over a medium heat, add chicken and cook for 4-5 minutes each side or until golden and tender. Place a chicken breast on the base of each roll. Top with tomato slices and endive leaves. Spoon over mayonnaise and cover with tops of rolls.

Serving suggestion: For a complete meal, serve with coleslaw and fresh fruit.

Serves 4

In winter use a vacuum flask to keep soups, stews or casseroles hot for office or school lunches.

TRI-POTATO SALAD

1730 kilojoules/410 Calories per serve – medium carbohydrate; low fat; high fibre

12 baby new potatoes
500 g/1 lb orange sweet potato, peeled and cubed
500 g/1 lb white sweet potato, peeled and cubed
1 small onion, chopped
250 g/8 oz reduced-fat-and-salt ham, chopped

MUSTARD HERB DRESSING
2 tablespoons snipped fresh chives
2 teaspoons wholegrain mustard
5 tablespoons reduced-fat mayonnaise
3 tablespoons low-fat natural yogurt

1 Boil, steam or microwave potatoes and orange and white sweet potatoes separately, until tender. Drain and keep warm.

2 Place onion and ham in a nonstick frying pan over a medium heat and cook for 3 minutes or until onion is soft.

3 Place potatoes in a bowl, add onion mixture and toss.

4 To make dressing, place chives, mustard, mayonnaise and yogurt in a bowl and mix to combine. Spoon over warm salad and toss. Serve salad warm.

Serving suggestion: A salad of oranges and onions tossed in Fast French Dressing (page 31) is a good accompaniment for this salad.

Serves 4

For those who have higher energy requirements, add some of the following to packed lunches: dried fruit and nut mix; vegetable sticks; healthy biscuits; slices or muffins; low-fat natural or fruit-flavoured yogurt; fruit juices; and cheese sticks.

The carbohydrate connection

Carbohydrate is stored in the body as glucose in the blood (blood sugar), and as glycogen in the liver and muscles. Glycogen, made up of units of glucose, is an important source of energy for active people. When glycogen stores are depleted, fatigue sets in and performance suffers. The amount of glycogen required depends on the duration, type and intensity of exercise.

To maintain adequate glycogen stores for training, active people should aim to consume 55-60 per cent of their energy requirements as carbohydrate. Endurance athletes need to aim for about 70 per cent.

Complex carbohydrate (starch) should make up most of the carbohydrate consumed. It sustains blood sugar levels more effectively than simple carbohydrate (sugars). Complex carbohydrate foods are also a better source of vitamins, minerals and fibre.
Sources: bread, breakfast cereal, rice, pasta, potato, dried peas and beans.

Simple carbohydrate (sugars) should supply less than 15 per cent of total carbohydrate intake.
Sources: sugar, honey, jam, confectionery, and soft drinks.

Carbohydrate (glycogen) loading:
Increasing or 'loading' glycogen stores is important for athletes taking part in endurance competitions which involve greater than 90 minutes of strenuous, uninterrupted effort. The 'extra' glycogen store helps to delay fatigue and enhance staying power. Glycogen loading also helps to prevent hypoglycaemia – low blood sugar.

In sports where speed, agility and flexibility are more important than stamina the extra weight of glycogen and the water that is stored with it (3 grams for each gram of glycogen), is likely to be detrimental. An adequate, rather than 'loaded' store is appropriate for these sports.

Loading up:
• Commence carbohydrate loading 3-4 days prior to competition.
• Increase carbohydrate intake to 70-85 per cent of energy (about 8-10 grams of carbohydrate per kilogram of bodyweight).
• Decrease training to reduce the use of muscle glycogen.

HYPOGLYCAEMIA
Endurance exercise can reduce blood sugar and glycogen stores to dangerously low levels. A low blood sugar level – hypoglycaemia – can cause symptoms such as dizziness, shakiness, faintness and confusion. In severe cases there is also risk of collapse.

• Sports such as marathons, triathalons and iron-man events require high levels of endurance.
• Other sports, like shot put, high jump and sprint events are based on repeated, short periods of non-endurance exercise.
• The vast majority of sports fall somewhere between these two extremes.
• The longer the duration of strenuous, uninterrupted effort the greater the endurance required.

CARBOHYDRATE COUNTER		
FOOD	**SERVE SIZE**	**CARBOHYDRATE (g)**
BREAD		
Wholemeal bread	1 slice	11
Raisin bread	1 slice	17
Lebanese or pitta bread	1 round	57
Wholemeal crispbread	2 biscuits	8.0
CEREALS		
Cornflakes	1 cup/30 g/1 oz	25
Muesli (untoasted)	½ cup/60 g/2 oz	33
Rolled oats (cooked)	1 cup/250 g/8 oz	22
FRUIT		
Orange	1 medium	12
Orange juice	1 cup/250 mL/8 fl oz	20
Pear	1 medium	19
Rock melon (cantaloupe)	1 cup/155 g/5 oz, diced	8
Sultanas	1 tablespoon	9
PASTA AND RICE (cooked)		
Egg pasta	200 g/6½ oz	51
Spinach pasta	200 g/6½ oz	55
Wholemeal pasta	200 g/6½ oz	49
Brown rice	1 cup/185 g/6 oz	57
White rice	1 cup/185 g/6 oz	53
VEGETABLES AND LEGUMES		
Cooked lentils	1 cup/155 g/5 oz	26
Potato	1 medium	16

MIGHTY
mains

VEGETARIAN PAN PIZZA

1300 kilojoules/310 Calories per serve – high carbohydrate; medium fat; high fibre

PIZZA BASE
15 g/^{1}/$_2$ oz fresh yeast
^{1}/$_2$ teaspoon sugar
^{1}/$_2$ cup/125 mL/4 fl oz lukewarm water
1^1/$_2$ cups/235 g/7^1/$_2$ oz wholemeal flour, sifted and husks returned
1 teaspoon olive oil

EGGPLANT AND HERB TOPPING
1 small eggplant (aubergine), thinly sliced
2 teaspoons olive oil
^{1}/$_3$ cup/90 mL/3 fl oz no-added-salt tomato sauce
1 teaspoon chopped fresh oregano
1 teaspoon chopped fresh basil
1 onion, finely sliced
1 red pepper, finely sliced
6 button mushrooms, finely sliced
200 g/6^1/$_2$ oz canned pineapple pieces, drained
4 black olives, pitted and sliced
60 g/2 oz grated reduced-fat mozzarella cheese

1 To make base, place yeast and sugar in a bowl and mix to combine. Stir in water, cover and stand in a warm draught-free place until mixture is foaming. Place flour in a separate bowl, stir in yeast mixture and oil and mix to make a soft dough.

2 Turn dough onto a lightly floured surface and knead for 5 minutes or until smooth and elastic. Place dough in a lightly oiled bowl, cover and stand in a warm draught-free place for 30 minutes, or until dough doubles in volume. Remove dough from bowl, knead on a lightly floured surface, then roll out to make a 25 cm/10 in circle. Place in a 25 cm/10 in nonstick frying pan.

3 To make topping, brush eggplant (aubergine) slices with oil and cook under a preheated hot grill for 3-4 minutes each side or until golden. Spread pizza base with tomato sauce then sprinkle with oregano and basil. Top with eggplant (aubergine), onion, red pepper, mushrooms, pineapple and olives. Sprinkle with cheese.

4 Cover pan and cook over a low heat for 35 minutes or until pizza crust is cooked. Place pizza under a preheated hot grill and cook for 3 minutes or until top is golden.

Serving suggestion: Cut pizza into wedges and serve with coleslaw or a green salad and crusty bread rolls.

Serves 4

This is a vegetarian pizza, but you can vary the topping according to what you have and what your favourite foods are. If you want to add some meat or fish you might like to use chopped reduced-fat-and-salt ham, or drained canned tuna in water in place of the eggplant (aubergine).

Minestrone Soup (page 24), Vegetarian Pan Pizza, Fish Cakes with Chilli Sauce (page 24)

Fish Cakes with Chilli Sauce

860 kilojoules/205 Calories per serve – low carbohydrate; low fat; medium fibre

500 g/1 lb boneless white fish fillets
1 cup/60 g/2 oz wholemeal
breadcrumbs, made from stale bread
2 spring onions, finely chopped
1 clove garlic, crushed
1 egg white
2 tablespoons low-fat natural yogurt
1 tablespoon lemon juice

CHILLI SAUCE
1 teaspoon olive oil
3 spring onions, chopped
$^1/_2$ red pepper, finely chopped
1 red chilli, seeded and finely chopped
440 g/14 oz canned no-added-salt
tomatoes, drained and chopped
1 cup/250 mL/8 fl oz no-added-salt
tomato purée

The uncooked fish cakes can be stored in the refrigerator for up to a day or frozen for up to 2 months.

1 Place fish in a food processor and process until smooth. Add breadcrumbs, spring onions, garlic, egg white, yogurt and lemon juice and process to combine.

2 Using wet hands, shape fish mixture into 8 patties. Heat a nonstick frying pan over a medium heat and cook patties for 2-3 minutes each side. Keep warm.

3 To make sauce, heat oil in a saucepan over a medium heat, add spring onions, red pepper and chilli and cook for 3-4 minutes. Add tomatoes and tomato purée, bring to the boil, then reduce heat and simmer uncovered, for 5 minutes or until sauce thickens.

Serving suggestion: Top patties with Chilli Sauce and accompany with brown rice and a crisp green salad. For a tasty meal serve the fish cakes in a wholemeal roll. Split the roll and toast cut sides. Fill roll with lettuce leaves, a fish cake and a spoonful of Chilli Sauce.

Serves 4

Minestrone Soup

855 kilojoules/205 Calories per serve – medium carbohydrate; low fat; high fibre

1 onion, chopped
3 cloves garlic, crushed
2 x 440 g/14 oz canned no-added-salt
tomatoes, undrained and chopped
2 zucchini (courgettes), diced
2 carrots, peeled and diced
1 large potato, diced
1 teaspoon dried oregano
2 teaspoons dried basil
freshly ground black pepper
4 cups/1 litre/1$^3/_4$ pt vegetable stock
315 g/10 oz canned red kidney beans,
rinsed and drained
155 g/5 oz macaroni, cooked and drained
1 tablespoon chopped fresh parsley
2 tablespoons grated parmesan cheese

Serve soup in warm bowls with crusty wholemeal bread rolls and a crisp green salad.

1 Place onion, garlic and 2 tablespoons of juice from tomatoes in a saucepan over a medium heat and cook for 2-3 minutes or until onion is soft. Add zucchini (courgettes), carrots, potato, oregano, basil and black pepper to taste and cook, stirring, for 5 minutes.

2 Stir in tomatoes and stock and bring to the boil. Reduce heat and simmer, uncovered, for 20 minutes.

3 Add red kidney beans, macaroni and parsley and cook over a low heat for 5 minutes or until heated through. Sprinkle with parmesan cheese.

Serves 4

CHILLI CON CARNE

2545 kilojoules/605 Calories per serve – low carbohydrate; medium fat; high fibre

2 onions, chopped
¹/₂ red pepper, finely chopped
2 cloves garlic, crushed
440 g/14 oz canned no-added-salt
tomatoes, drained, chopped and
1 tablespoon juice reserved
500 g/1 lb lean minced beef
315 g/10 oz canned red kidney beans,
rinsed and drained
1 teaspoon ground cumin
1 teaspoon ground coriander
¹/₂ teaspoon chilli powder
¹/₂ cup/125 mL/4 fl oz beef stock
2 tablespoons no-added-salt tomato
paste (purée)

CORN BREAD
1 cup/185 g/6 oz polenta (corn meal)
³/₄ cup/90 g/3 oz self-raising flour,
sifted
¹/₂ teaspoon sugar
1 cup/250 mL/8 fl oz skim milk
1 egg
1 tablespoon polyunsaturated
margarine, melted

1 Place onions, red pepper, garlic and
reserved juice from tomatoes in a
nonstick frying pan over a medium heat
and cook for 4-5 minutes. Stir in beef
and cook for 10 minutes. Add tomatoes,
red kidney beans, cumin, coriander,
chilli powder, stock and tomato paste
(purée) and bring to the boil. Reduce
heat and simmer for 25 minutes or
until mixture reduces and thickens.

2 To make Corn Bread, combine
polenta (corn meal), flour and sugar in
a bowl. Whisk together milk, egg and
margarine, then stir into the polenta
mixture. Mix to combine.

3 Spread mixture into a greased
20 cm/8 in round cake pan and bake for
15-20 minutes, or until bread is golden.
Serve warm with Chilli con Carne.

Serves 4

Oven temperature
180°C, 350°F, Gas 4

Polenta (corn meal) is a
maize flour much used in
Italy for both savoury and
sweet dishes. It is available
from most supermarkets,
Italian and health food
shops. The grainy texture of
cooked polenta (corn
meal) may surprise you at
first, but that's how it's meant
to be.

Chilli con Carne

GOLDEN BUTTERNUT SOUP

515 kilojoules/125 Calories per serve – high carbohydrate; low fat; medium fibre

1 onion, chopped
1 clove garlic, crushed
4 cups/1 litre/1³/₄ pt chicken or
vegetable stock
750 g/1¹/₂ lb butternut pumpkin,
peeled and sliced
2 potatoes, peeled and sliced
¹/₂ teaspoon dried marjoram
¹/₂ teaspoon grated nutmeg
freshly ground black pepper
3 tablespoons buttermilk

1   Place onion, garlic and 2 tablespoons stock in a saucepan over a medium heat and cook for 2-3 minutes or until onion is soft. Add remaining stock, pumpkin, potatoes, marjoram, nutmeg and black pepper to taste and cook, stirring occasionally, for 25 minutes, or until pumpkin and potato are tender. Stir in buttermilk. Cool slightly.

2   Purée soup, in batches, in a food processor or blender.

3   Return soup to a clean saucepan and heat gently, do not allow to boil or soup will curdle.

Serving suggestion: Pour soup into large mugs or warm bowls, sprinkle with snipped fresh chives and serve with wholegrain bread rolls.

Serves 4

This soup can be stored in the refrigerator for up to 3 days and reheated as required in a saucepan or in the microwave. In the microwave reheat the soup in the serving mugs. One serving will take 2-3 minutes to reheat on HIGH (100%) – depending on the serving size.

QUICK AND EASY QUICHE

1385 kilojoules/330 Calories per serve – low carbohydrate; high fat; high fibre

15 g/¹/₂ oz polyunsaturated
margarine, melted
8 slices wholegrain bread,
crusts removed

VEGETABLE FILLING
155 g/5 oz broccoli, cut into florets
125 g/4 oz canned sweet corn
kernels, drained
125 g/4 oz button mushrooms, sliced
¹/₂ red pepper, chopped
4 eggs, lightly beaten
³/₄ cup/185 mL/6 fl oz skim milk
¹/₂ cup/60 g/2 oz grated reduced-fat
cheddar cheese
freshly ground black pepper

1   Brush a 23 cm/9 in flan dish with margarine. Line dish with bread, trimming slices to fit base and sides.

2   To make filling, arrange broccoli, sweet corn, mushrooms and red pepper in bread case. Place eggs and milk in a bowl and whisk to combine. Pour egg mixture over vegetables, sprinkle with cheese and black pepper to taste. Bake for 30-35 minutes or until filling is firm.

Serving suggestion: Delicious served hot, warm or cold with steamed vegetables of your choice or a tossed salad.

Serves 4

Oven temperature
180°C, 350°F, Gas 4

Any vegetables of your choice can be used in this quiche – it is a good way to use up odds and ends in the vegetable bin. Longer cooking vegetables such as carrots, potatoes and parsnips should be partially cooked first.

PORK WITH RED WINE SAUCE

1150 kilojoules/275 Calories per serve - low carbohydrate; high fat; low fibre

2 small pork fillets, each about
250 g/8 oz, trimmed of visible fat
1 tablespoon honey, warmed
1 tablespoon Worcestershire sauce
1 tablespoon red wine

RED WINE SAUCE
1 small onion, chopped
$^1/_2$ stalk celery, chopped
1 teaspoon sweet fruit chutney
1 cup/250 mL/8 fl oz chicken stock
$^1/_4$ cup/60 mL/2 fl oz red wine
2 teaspoons polyunsaturated
margarine
2 teaspoons plain flour
185 g/6 oz button mushrooms, sliced

1   Place fillets in a shallow glass or
ceramic dish. Combine honey,
Worcestershire sauce and wine, pour
over fillets and marinate, turning
occasionally, for 15-20 minutes. Drain
pork and cook on a preheated hot
barbecue or grill, turning and brushing
with marinade several times, for
10-15 minutes or until pork is cooked
to your liking.

2   To make sauce, place onion, celery,
chutney, stock and wine in a saucepan
over a low heat and cook, stirring, for
5 minutes, or until liquid reduces by
half. Strain and set aside.

3   Melt margarine in a clean saucepan
over a medium heat, stir in flour and
cook for 1 minute. Remove pan from
heat and gradually whisk in red wine
mixture. Add mushrooms and cook,
stirring constantly, for 5 minutes or
until sauce boils and thickens.

Serving suggestion: Cut pork into
thick slices, spoon sauce over and serve
with a green salad or vegetables of your
choice and boiled new potatoes.

Serves 4

ISLAND HOPPING DRESSING

50 kilojoules/10 Calories per serve – low carbohydrate; negligible fat; nil fibre

4 tablespoons low-fat natural yogurt
2 tablespoons skim milk
1 tablespoon no-added-salt tomato
paste (purée)
1 tablespoon red wine vinegar
3 drops Tabasco sauce

Place yogurt, milk, tomato paste
(purée), vinegar and Tabasco sauce in a
screwtop jar and shake to combine.

Makes 1 cup/250 mL/8 fl oz

EGGPLANT LASAGNE

1200 kilojoules/285 Calories per serve – low carbohydrate; high fat; medium fibre

$^1/_4$ cup/60 mL/2 fl oz lemon juice
1 tablespoon olive oil
$^1/_2$ teaspoon cracked black pepper
1 large eggplant (aubergine), about
500 g/1 lb, halved lengthways and cut
into 5 mm/$^1/_4$ in thick slices
$^1/_2$ cup/30 g/1 oz wholemeal
breadcrumbs, made from stale bread
3 tablespoons grated parmesan cheese
1 large onion, chopped
2 cloves garlic, crushed
1 teaspoon dried oregano
1 teaspoon dried basil
pinch cayenne pepper
440 g/14 oz canned no-added-salt
tomatoes, drained, chopped and
1 tablespoon juice reserved
$^3/_4$ cup/185 mL/6 fl oz no-added-salt
tomato purée
2 tablespoons white wine
6 wholemeal instant lasagne sheets
$^3/_4$ cup/185 g/6 oz reduced-fat ricotta
cheese
3 tablespoons grated reduced-fat
mozzarella cheese

1   Combine lemon juice, oil and black pepper and use to brush eggplant (aubergine) slices. Cook eggplant (aubergine) under a preheated hot grill for 3-4 minutes each side or until golden. Combine breadcrumbs and parmesan cheese and set aside.

2   Place onion, garlic and reserved tomato juice in a nonstick frying pan over a medium heat and cook for 2-3 minutes. Add oregano, basil, cayenne pepper, tomatoes, tomato purée and wine and cook, stirring, for 5 minutes.

3   Spread one-third of the tomato mixture over base of a 15 x 25 cm/ 6 x 10 in ovenproof dish. Top with 3 lasagne sheets and half of the breadcrumb mixture, then cover with a layer of eggplant. Top with half the ricotta cheese. Repeat layers, ending with a layer of tomato mixture. Sprinkle with mozzarella cheese and bake for 45 minutes.

Serves 4

Oven temperature
180°C, 350°F, Gas 4

For a complete meal serve with a tossed green salad or steamed green vegetables of your choice.

Eggplant Lasagne

PESTO DRESSING

185 kilojoules/45 Calories per serve – low carbohydrate; high fat; negligible fibre

60 g/2 oz fresh basil leaves
2 tablespoons grated parmesan cheese
1 tablespoon pine nuts, toasted
2 cloves garlic, chopped
4 tablespoons white vinegar
2 tablespoons polyunsaturated vegetable oil

Place basil, parmesan cheese, pine nuts, garlic, vinegar and oil in a food processor or blender and process until smooth.

Makes 1 cup/250 mL/8 fl oz

Use as a dressing on a pasta salad. Also good as a dip for raw or lightly steamed vegetables and tossed through hot pasta.

TANGY CUCUMBER DRESSING

25 kilojoules/6 Calories per serve – negligible carbohydrate; negligible fat; negligible fibre

1 small cucumber, seeded and finely chopped
1 tablespoon wholegrain mustard
1 cup/200 g/6½ oz low-fat natural yogurt

Place cucumber, mustard and yogurt in a bowl and mix to combine.

Makes 1½ cups/375 mL/12 fl oz

Use as a dressing for potato salad, or as a dip for raw or lightly cooked vegetables.

Oriental Dressing, Fast French Dressing, Island Hopping Dressing (page 28), Pesto Dressing, Tangy Cucumber Dressing

ORIENTAL DRESSING

155 kilojoules/35 Calories per serve – negligible carbohydrate; high fat; negligible fibre

2 teaspoons grated fresh ginger
1 tablespoon sesame seeds
1 small fresh red chilli, finely chopped
2 tablespoons polyunsaturated
vegetable oil
1 tablespoon sweet sherry
1 tablespoon reduced-salt soy sauce
¹/₂ teaspoon sesame oil

Place ginger, sesame seeds, chilli, vegetable oil, sherry, soy sauce and sesame oil in a screwtop jar and shake to combine.

Makes 1 cup/250 mL/8 fl oz

Use as a dressing on a salad made from Chinese noodles, pasta or lettuce. Also delicious tossed through hot noodles for a quick flavour booster.

FAST FRENCH DRESSING

115 kilojoules/25 Calories per serve – negligible carbohydrate; high fat; negligible fibre

1 tablespoon chopped fresh
flat-leaf parsley
1 tablespoon snipped fresh chives
1 tablespoon chopped fresh tarragon
¹/₂ teaspoon sugar
¹/₄ teaspoon dry mustard
4 tablespoons lemon or lime juice
4 tablespoons white wine vinegar
2 tablespoons olive oil

Place parsley, chives, tarragon, sugar, mustard, lemon or lime juice, vinegar and oil in a screwtop jar and shake to combine.

Makes 1 cup/250 mL/8 fl oz

Use as a dressing on coleslaw, lettuce or hot potato salad.

VEGETABLE AND TOFU STIR-FRY

860 kilojoules/205 Calories per serve – low carbohydrate; high fat; medium fibre

500 g/1 lb tofu, cut into small cubes
1 fresh red chilli, finely chopped
2 tablespoons reduced-salt soy sauce
2 teaspoons honey, warmed
1 teaspoon sesame oil
2 carrots, peeled
2 zucchini (courgettes)
1 small eggplant (aubergine)
1 parsnip
2 teaspoons polyunsaturated
vegetable oil
2 onions, cut into eighths
2 tablespoons sesame seeds

1 Place tofu, chilli, soy sauce, honey and sesame oil in a bowl and marinate for 15-20 minutes.

2 Using a wide-bladed vegetable peeler, peel lengthwise strips from carrots, zucchini (courgettes), eggplant (aubergine) and parsnip.

3 Heat oil in a wok or frying pan over a medium heat, add onions and stir-fry for 3 minutes or until soft. Add carrots, zucchini (courgettes), eggplant (aubergine), parsnip and sesame seeds and stir-fry for 6-8 minutes, or until vegetables are tender crisp.

4 Add tofu and marinade to pan and stir-fry for 2 minutes or until tofu is heated through.

Serves 4

Carbohydrate foods have long had the reputation for making people fat. Carbohydrates actually contain less energy than fats and are less readily converted to fat in the body. Whilst excessive carbohydrate intake will eventually increase weight, fat will do it more readily.
1 g fat = 37 kJ/9 Cals
1 g carbohydrate = 16 kJ/4 Cals

HOT CHICKEN CURRY

855 kilojoules/205 Calories per serve – high carbohydrate; low fat; medium fibre

10 new potatoes, peeled and halved
2 onions, cut into eighths
1 clove garlic, crushed
$^1/_2$ teaspoon hot curry paste
3 teaspoons curry powder
2 teaspoons ground cumin
440 g/14 oz canned no-added-salt tomatoes, undrained and mashed
1 cup/250 mL/8 fl oz chicken stock
4 tablespoons no-added-salt tomato purée
2 tablespoons dry white wine
2 tablespoons mango chutney
2 boneless chicken breast fillets, cut into 2 cm/$^3/_4$ in cubes
1 tablespoon chopped fresh coriander

1 Boil, steam or microwave potatoes until just tender. Cool.

2 Place onions, garlic, curry paste and 1 tablespoon of juice from tomatoes in a saucepan over a medium heat and cook for 2-3 minutes or until onion is soft.

3 Combine curry powder, cumin, tomatoes, stock, tomato purée, wine and chutney. Stir into onion mixture and cook for 2-3 minutes. Add chicken and potatoes and cook over a low heat for 5 minutes or until chicken is tender. Just prior to serving, sprinkle with coriander.

Serves 4

Although active people lose salt in sweat, the body adapts to these increased losses and conserves salt by decreasing its concentration in sweat. Adequate salt can therefore be obtained without the addition of salt to food.

VEAL GOULASH

1005 kilojoules/240 Calories per serve – low carbohydrate; low fat; medium fibre

**4 x 1 cm/¹/₂ in thick veal steaks, each
about 125 g/4 oz, trimmed of visible fat
2 tablespoons plain flour
1 tablespoon paprika
¹/₂ teaspoon ground black pepper
2 teaspoons olive oil
2 onions, chopped
125 g/4 oz button mushrooms, sliced
2 cloves garlic, crushed
¹/₂ cup/125 mL/4 fl oz no-added-salt
tomato purée
¹/₂ cup/125 mL/4 fl oz beef stock
2 tablespoons sweet sherry
125 g/4 oz frozen peas
3 tablespoons low-fat natural yogurt
2 tablespoons chopped fresh parsley**

Stir in tomato purée, stock and sherry
and bring to the boil. Reduce heat and
simmer, uncovered, for 20 minutes.

3 Return veal to pan, add peas, and
cook for 5 minutes or until heated
through. Remove pan from heat and
stir in yogurt and parsley.

Serving suggestion: For a balanced
meal serve with brown rice and a green
salad, or vegetables such as pumpkin
and beans.

Serves 4

This goulash is also delicious
made with lean lamb.

1 Cut veal into 2 cm/³/₄ in pieces.
Place flour, paprika and black pepper in
a plastic food bag, add veal and shake
to coat evenly. Shake off excess flour.

2 Heat oil in a saucepan over a high
heat, add veal and cook, turning several
times, for 3-4 minutes or until brown.
Remove from pan and set aside. Add
onions, mushrooms and garlic and cook
for 2-3 minutes or until onion is soft.

Hot Chicken Curry

RICE PIE

1145 kilojoules/335 Calories per serve – high carbohydrate; low fat; high fibre

Oven temperature
180°C, 350°F, Gas 4

1 cup/220 g/7 oz brown rice, cooked
2 tablespoons grated parmesan cheese
¼ teaspoon chilli powder
2 egg whites

SWEET POTATO FILLING
750 g/1½ lb sweet potato, peeled,
cooked and mashed
2 tablespoons snipped fresh chives
½ teaspoon grated nutmeg
½ teaspoon ground cumin
2 eggs, lightly beaten

1 Place rice, parmesan cheese, chilli powder and egg whites in a bowl and mix to combine. Press mixture into a lightly greased 20 cm/8 in pie plate.

2 To make filling, place sweet potato, chives, nutmeg, cumin and eggs in a bowl and mix to combine. Spoon mixture into prepared pie plate and bake for 20-25 minutes or until filling is firm.

Serving suggestion: This easy pie can be served hot, warm or cold. For a complete meal just add a tossed green salad or coleslaw.

Serves 4

With its high-carbohydrate and low-fat content, small slices of this pie make an ideal snack.

SPEEDY SALMON RISSOLES

1405 kilojoules/335 Calories per serve – low carbohydrate; medium fat; medium fibre

3 large potatoes, cooked and mashed
440 g/14 oz canned no-added-salt pink
salmon, drained and flaked
155 g/5 oz grated pumpkin
3 spring onions, chopped
1 tablespoon German mustard
1 tablespoon low-fat natural yogurt
1 egg white
2 teaspoons lemon juice
2 cups/125 g/4 oz wholemeal
breadcrumbs, made from stale bread
2 teaspoons polyunsaturated
vegetable oil

1 Place potatoes, salmon, pumpkin, spring onions, mustard, yogurt, egg white and lemon juice in a bowl and mix to combine. Shape mixture into eight patties and roll in breadcrumbs to coat. Place patties on a plate lined with plastic food wrap and chill for 30 minutes.

2 Heat oil in a nonstick frying pan over a medium heat, add patties and cook for 3-4 minutes each side or until golden.

Serving suggestion: Accompany with a fresh salad and crusty bread.

Serves 4

Rice Pie, Vegetable and Tofu Stir-fry (page 32),
Veal Goulash (page 33)

SAVOURY-TOPPED POTATOES

8 potatoes, scrubbed

1 Boil, steam or microwave potatoes until tender.

2 Cut a cross in the top of each potato and press to open out. Divide topping of your choice (see below) between potatoes and place under a preheated hot grill for 4-5 minutes, if necessary, to warm filling.

Serves 4

CHEESE AND CHIVE TOPPING

790 kilojoules/190 Calories per serve (includes potatoes) – low carbohydrate; medium fat; medium fibre

³/₄ cup/185 g/6 oz reduced-fat ricotta cheese
4 tablespoons grated reduced-fat cheddar cheese
2 tablespoons snipped fresh chives
freshly ground black pepper

Place ricotta and cheddar cheeses, chives, and black pepper to taste in a bowl and mix to combine.

Serves 4

CHEESY SOYA BEAN TOPPING

995 kilojoules/235 Calories per serve (includes potatoes) – medium carbohydrate; medium fat; high fibre

1 cup/250 mL/8 fl oz skim milk
2 tablespoons cornflour
375 g/12 oz canned soya beans, drained
¹/₂ cup/60 g/2 oz grated reduced-fat cheddar cheese
2 tablespoons grated parmesan cheese
¹/₄ teaspoon grated nutmeg
1 tablespoon chopped fresh parsley
freshly ground black pepper

Gently heat ³/₄ cup/185 mL/6 fl oz milk in a saucepan, without boiling, for 3-4 minutes. Combine cornflour with remaining milk and stir into pan. Cook, stirring constantly, until sauce thickens. Stir in soya beans, cheddar and parmesan cheeses and nutmeg and cook for 2-3 minutes or until heated through. Stir in parsley and black pepper to taste.

Serves 4

LEBANESE PIZZA

1515 kilojoules/360 Calories per serve – low carbohydrate; high fat; medium fibre

1 cup/185 g/6 oz burghul
(cracked wheat)
1 onion, chopped
1 clove garlic, crushed
500 g/1 lb lean minced lamb
1 tablespoon chopped fresh mint
½ teaspoon dried mixed herbs
½ teaspoon chilli powder
1 tablespoon lemon juice

TOMATO AND HUMMUS TOPPING
¾ cup/220 g/7 oz hummus
2 tomatoes, sliced
8 spinach leaves, blanched and
chopped
3 tablespoons pine nuts
4 tablespoons grated low-fat
cheddar cheese

1   Place burghul (cracked wheat) in a bowl. Pour over 2 cups/500 mL/16 fl oz hot water and soak for 10-15 minutes. Drain burghul (cracked wheat) and set aside.

2   Place onion and garlic in a nonstick frying pan over a medium heat and cook, stirring, for 3 minutes or until onion is soft. Add onion mixture, lamb, mint, mixed herbs, chilli powder and lemon juice to burghul (cracked wheat) and mix to combine.

3   Press meat mixture into a 30 cm/12 in pizza tray and bake for 20 minutes or until base is firm. Drain off any juices.

4   To make topping, spread meat base with hummus then top with tomato slices and spinach. Sprinkle with pine nuts and cheese and cook under a preheated hot grill for 3-4 minutes or until cheese melts.

Serving suggestion: Cut pizza into wedges and serve with crusty bread and a salad.

Serves 6

Oven temperature
180°C, 350°F, Gas 4

During competition 'ultra' endurance athletes may benefit from sports drinks which contain small amounts of salt. Salt tablets are not recommended as they can cause gastric upset.

GINGER 'N' FRUIT COOKIES

300 kilojoules/70 Calories per serve – high carbohydrate; medium fat; low fibre

After training try to get home quickly; dawdling in the change room wastes time that could be spent in the kitchen.

1¹/₂ cups/235 g/7¹/₂ oz wholemeal self-raising flour, sifted and husks returned
¹/₄ cup/45 g g/1¹/₂ oz brown sugar
3 tablespoons dried mixed fruit, chopped
1 tablespoon chopped glacé ginger
3 egg whites, lightly beaten
¹/₃ cup/90 mL/3 fl oz skim milk
2 tablespoons olive oil
9 glacé cherries, halved

1 Place flour, sugar, fruit and ginger in a bowl and mix to combine.

2 Gradually stir in egg whites, milk and oil and mix well.

3 Place spoonfuls of mixture on a lightly greased baking tray, top with a cherry half and bake for 12-15 minutes or until golden. Transfer to wire racks to cool.

Makes 18

A variety of No Fussin' Muffins, Ginger 'n' Fruit Cookies

No Fussin' Muffins

504 kilojoules/120 Calories per serve (basic recipe) – medium carbohydrate; medium fat; medium fibre

1³/4 cups/280 g/9 oz wholemeal
self-raising flour, sifted and
husks returned
¹/2 cup/90 g/3 oz brown sugar
1 teaspoon baking powder
³/4 cup/185 mL/6 fl oz skim milk
1 egg, lightly beaten
3 tablespoons polyunsaturated
margarine, melted

1 Combine flour, sugar and baking
powder in a bowl. Stir in milk and egg,
then add margarine and mix well.

2 Spoon mixture into 12 lightly
greased muffin tins and bake for
20-25 minutes or until cooked when
tested with a skewer and golden.

Carrot and Walnut Muffins: Stir
155 g/5 oz grated carrot, 3 tablespoons
chopped walnuts and ¹/2 teaspoon
ground cinnamon into basic mixture.

Almond and Ginger Muffins: Stir
3 tablespoons ground almonds,
2 tablespoons finely chopped glacé
ginger and 2 teaspoons grated orange
rind into basic mixture.

Cranberry Muffins: Stir 170 g/5¹/2 oz
cranberry sauce into basic mixture.

Blueberry Muffins: Drain 440 g/14 oz
canned blueberries and stir into basic
mixture. Sprinkle each muffin with a
little coffee sugar before cooking.

Banana and Pecan Muffins: Mash
3 ripe bananas and stir into basic
mixture with 3 tablespoons chopped
pecan nuts. Combine 3 tablespoons
brown sugar, 3 tablespoons finely
chopped pecans and 1 teaspoon ground
cinnamon and sprinkle over muffins
before cooking.

Makes 12

Oven temperature
180°C, 350°F, Gas 4

Do a little extra cooking
during the weekend when
you have more time.
Choose things you can
freeze and reheat quickly.
These muffins reheat in the
microwave in 30-45 seconds.

Muesli Slice

390 kilojoules/95 Calories per serve – low carbohydrate; high fat; low fibre

Oven temperature
160°C, 325°F, Gas 3

If living in a shared house of busy people, organise a roster system for the cooking. Ideally you get a meal cooked for you on the nights you are home latest.

60 g/2 oz polyunsaturated margarine
3 tablespoons honey
1 cup/200 g/6½ oz low-fat natural yogurt
2 eggs, lightly beaten
1 cup/250 g/8 oz reduced-fat ricotta cheese, drained
1 cup/155 g/5 oz wholemeal flour, sifted and husks returned
125 g/4 oz raisins, chopped
½ cup/45 g/1½ oz desiccated coconut
45 g/1½ oz flaked almonds
3 tablespoons sesame seeds

1 Place margarine and honey in a bowl and beat to combine. Gradually mix in yogurt and eggs, then stir in ricotta cheese, flour, raisins, coconut, almonds and sesame seeds.

2 Pour mixture into a lightly greased and lined shallow 18 x 28 cm/7 x 11 in cake tin and bake for 35-40 minutes or until firm and golden brown. Cool slice in tin, then cut into squares.

Makes 24

Speedy Date Slice

715 kilojoules/170 Calories per serve – high carbohydrate; low fat; low fibre

Oven temperature
180°C, 350°F, Gas 4

Children are usually the hungriest straight after school. Organise a substantial snack at this time, prior to training. A combination of soups, sandwiches, yogurts, fruits (fresh, dried or canned), fruit juices, cheese sticks and homemade muffins are all good snack foods. A small snack, drink or a part of dinner can be consumed on the way home.

90 g/3 oz polyunsaturated margarine
¾ cup/185 g/6 oz raw sugar
1 egg
155 g/5 oz chopped dried dates
1 cup/125 g/4 oz self-raising flour
½ cup/60 g/2 oz muesli
2 tablespoons sunflower seeds
2 tablespoons chopped green pumpkin seeds
1 tablespoon poppy seeds
½ cup/100 g/3½ oz low-fat natural yogurt

LEMON ICING
2 teaspoons polyunsaturated margarine
2 tablespoons hot water
4 tablespoons lemon juice
2 cups/315 g/10 oz icing sugar, sifted

1 Place margarine and sugar in a bowl and beat until light and fluffy. Beat in egg, then stir in dates, flour, muesli, sunflower seeds, pumpkin seeds, poppy seeds and yogurt.

2 Spoon mixture into a lightly greased and lined shallow 18 x 28 cm/7 x 11 in cake tin and bake for 25 minutes or until firm and golden. Cool in tin.

3 To make icing, stir margarine into hot water until melted, then stir in lemon juice. Add icing sugar and beat until smooth. Spread evenly over cooled slice. Allow icing to set then cut into fingers or squares.

Makes 24

Wholehearted Rockcakes (page 42), Speedy Date Slice, Oaty Biscuits (page 42), Muesli Slice

OATY BISCUITS

665 kilojoules/160 Calories per serve – high carbohydrate; medium fat; low fibre

Oven temperature
180°C, 350°F, Gas 4

Loss of appetite may be related to overtraining or medical problems. These should be investigated if the lack of appetite persists. Personal problems or pressures can also affect appetite, in either direction. Coaches, parents or spouses should take time to talk over issues on a regular basis.

60 g/2 oz polyunsaturated margarine
3 tablespoons brown sugar
1 teaspoon vanilla essence
1 egg
1 cup/90 g/3 oz rolled oats
¹/₂ cup/75 g/2¹/₂ oz wholemeal self-raising flour, sifted and husks returned
3 tablespoons chopped pecans
3 tablespoons chopped dates
3 tablespoons wheat germ

PINK ICING
2 teaspoons polyunsaturated margarine
3 tablespoons hot water
1 cup/155 g/5 oz icing sugar, sifted
few drops pink food colouring

1 Place margarine in a bowl and beat until light and fluffy. Add sugar and vanilla essence and beat to combine. Beat in egg.

2 Stir in oats, flour, pecans, dates and wheat germ and mix well.

3 Place spoonfuls of mixture on lightly greased baking trays and bake for 10 minutes or until golden. Transfer to wire racks to cool.

4 To make icing, stir margarine into hot water until melted. Add icing sugar and beat until smooth. Colour with food colouring and place a little icing on each biscuit.

Makes 15

WHOLEHEARTED ROCKCAKES

500 kilojoules/120 Calories per serve – medium carbohydrate; high fat; low fibre

Oven temperature
180°C, 350°F, Gas 4

Try some of the recipes from the drinks section (page 48-50) so that you can maintain some energy with liquid food. Commercial sports drinks are also available if you do not have time to make your own.

2 cups/315 g/10 oz wholemeal self-raising flour, sifted and husks returned
¹/₃ cup/90 oz/3 oz raw sugar
¹/₂ teaspoon ground cinnamon
125 g/4 oz polyunsaturated margarine
125 g/4 oz raisins, chopped
30 g/1 oz dried apples, chopped
1 egg, lightly beaten
4 tablespoons skim milk

1 Place flour, sugar and cinnamon in a bowl. Using fingertips rub in margarine. Stir in raisins and apples, then gradually add egg and enough milk to make a thick dough.

2 Drop large spoonfuls of mixture onto lightly greased baking trays and bake for 12-15 minutes or until cooked and golden.

Makes 20

Takeaway tucker

Fast foods may be fast to eat but they definitely do not make you fast on the athletic field! Unfortunately, fast food is generally high in fat, cholesterol and salt. Active people with hearty appetites can eat large quantities of fast food without getting full, as there is usually little complex carbohydrate or fibre to fill them up. The occasional indulgence is not a problem, providing it is not a precompetition meal. Follow these guidelines for the best fast food and restaurant choices.

THE TAKEAWAY BAR

Do order: Plain hamburgers with salad, steak sandwiches, barbecue chicken (skin removed), thick crust pizza (no extra cheese), sandwiches, rolls, pocket bread (preferably wholemeal), jacket potatoes with topping (but no sour cream), fruit, fruit salads, dried fruit, low-fat yogurts, smoothies, juices, plain mineral water, plain scones, fruit buns, wholemeal muffins.

Best avoided: French fries, any battered food such as chicken, fish or sausages, crumbed meats, chicko rolls, pies, sausage rolls, fatty meats such as devon or salami, cream cakes or desserts, confectionery or crisps.

ITALIAN

Do order: Vegetable antipasto, minestrone or vegetable soup, grissini bread sticks, crusty bread, calamari salad, prosciutto and melon, ravioli, tortellini, spaghetti, fettuccine or other pasta with any of the following sauces – napolitana (tomato); marinara (seafood); bolognaise (meat); primavera (vegetable); putanesca (tomato, vegetable and olives); chicken cacciatore, grilled garlic chicken, veal scallopine, osso bucco, pizza with thick crust (avoid too much cheese), gelato and fresh fruits.

Best avoided: Garlic or herb bread, salami, peperoni, any fried food, cannelloni, lasagne, pasta with cream sauces, saltimbocca (veal with ham and cheese), zabaglione and cassata.

CHINESE

Do order: Clear short soups with or without wontons or dumplings, crab and corn soup, steamed dim sims or wontons, pork and lettuce rolls, satay prawns, steamed fish with black bean sauce, steamed rice, combination vegetables, stir-fry dishes with lean meat, chicken or pork, chow mein dishes, chop suey dishes, Mongolian hot pot, lychees and Chinese tea.

Best avoided: Any deep-fried foods, crisp skin chicken, chicken in lemon sauce, sweet and sour dishes, fried rice, fried noodles, Peking duck, pork spare ribs, deep-fried whole fish and chicken wings.

MIDDLE EASTERN

Do order: Hummus, eggplant dip, flatbread, pitta bread, tabbouleh, kafta, shish kebabs, souvlaki, shawarma or doner kebab, kibbi, rice-stuffed marrow or zucchini (courgettes), yogurt and cucumber dip.

Best avoided: Falafel, spicy sausages, baklava, bread with oil or melted butter.

COUNTDOWN TO competition

Nutrition strategies used in competition can either make or break a performance! Your needs are dictated by the type and duration of the sport you participate in.

Those competing in endurance events benefit from a higher-than-normal glycogen store. This can be achieved by carbohydrate loading (page 21). For events shorter than this, an adequate glycogen store can be achieved in 24-36 hours if training is tapered and a high-carbohydrate diet is eaten. The precompetition meal and what to eat and/or drink during events should all be planned well before competition. Practise competition strategies in training sessions. Time spent planning will help ensure that nutrition strategies run smoothly on competition day.

PRECOMPETITION MEALS

Eat your pre-event meal 2-4 hours before you are due to compete. Eating closer to the event will divert the blood supply to the digestive system and away from the working muscles. Use the following tips and experiment with different meals to find out what works best.

- Make that pre-event meal a low-fat occasion – fat slows digestion.
- Top up glycogen stores with high-carbohydrate foods.
- Avoid alcohol 24-48 hours prior to competition.
- Prevent dehydration with a moderate protein intake and no added salt. Excess protein and salt increases urine output.
- Maintain hydration – drink fluids liberally – at least 2 glasses/ 500 mL/16 fl oz 30 minutes prior to competition. It is recommended that endurance athletes increase fluid intake up to 24 hours prior to competition.
- Have your meal – but drink it! This way you can maintain your energy with liquid food.

WIN THE WAITING GAME

Many sporting competitions such as gymnastics, dancing eisteddfods, track and field events and swimming carnivals are organised around several heats or trials which may extend over a whole day. Under these circumstances it is important to keep fluid and glycogen stores up. To do this effectively, a competition 'eating strategy' needs to be planned.

- Drinks are best for short breaks – juices, cordials, flat soft drinks or glucose polymer drinks. They help replace fluid and carbohydrate. For very short breaks, plain water is best.
- In longer breaks eat light carbohydrate-rich foods. Try canned, dried or ripe, peeled fruits; jelly; low-fat yogurts or custards; sandwiches with lean meat or, high-carbohydrate fillings such as banana, honey and jam. The main aim is light, high-carbohydrate, low-fat foods or fluids.
- Liquid meals digest faster than solids.
- Always take some food or drink with you – sporting venues usually do not carry suitable foods for between events.
- Little and often is a good philosophy. This helps to keep hunger at bay and prevents that bloated feeling.
- Fluids are a priority and are easily forgotten when you are nervous.
- Eating and drinking between events can be difficult for those who are unaccustomed to it. The best place to practise is at training. After a while it will all come naturally.

PUTTING A STOP TO THE PIT STOP

While high-fibre diets are healthy and are recommended for most people, a high-fibre intake prior to competition can get the bowels working overtime – particularly if you get nervous. Having liquid meals or a reduced-fibre diet can help to prevent excessive 'pit stops'. After competition, a high-fibre diet can be resumed.

For some athletes, particularly endurance runners, frequent 'pit stops' can interfere with their regular training. These athletes consume large amounts of kilojoules (calories) from foods rich in carbohydrate and fibre so their usual fibre intake tends to be fairly high and sometimes higher than their bowel can cope with! These athletes will train more comfortably by reducing fibre intake a little. This can be done by substituting some of the high-fibre foods with the following:

- Choose white or light brown breads instead of heavy wholemeal.
- Choose white rice or pasta.
- Avoid bran-based cereals and unprocessed bran.
- Peel fruits before eating.
- Do not go overboard with the very high-fibre foods, such as dried peas, beans and nuts.
- Give preference to high-carbohydrate (starchy) vegetables like potatoes.

Precompetition menu planner

Make the most of what you eat when it's a week before you compete. Use this seven-day menu planner as a guide.

DAY 1

Breakfast
Fruit juice
Rolled oats with low-fat milk
Peaches and Cream Muffins (page 11)

Lunch
Golden Butternut Soup (page 26)
Wholemeal bread roll spread thinly with polyunsaturated margarine, reduced-fat spread or butter
Soya Bean-topped Potatoes (page 36)
Green salad
Fresh fruit
Natural mineral water

Dinner
Honey Beef (page 66)
Steamed brown rice
Green salad with Oriental Dressing (page 31)
Wholemeal bread roll spread thinly with polyunsaturated margarine, reduced-fat spread or butter
Crêpe Escapes (page 76)

Snacks
1 piece fresh fruit
200 g/6^1/$_2$ oz carton low-fat yogurt
1 No Fussin' Muffin (page 39)
1 Smashing Smoothie (page 48)

DAY 2

Breakfast
^{1}/$_2$ small rock melon (cantaloupe) sprinkled with sultanas
Vegetable Hash Browns (page 12)
2 slices wholemeal toast or bread spread thinly with polyunsaturated margarine, reduced-fat spread or butter
Shake It Up milkshake (page 50)

Lunch
Fettuccine Vegetable Medley (page 58)
1 cup fruit salad
200 g/6^1/$_2$ oz carton low-fat yogurt
Fruit juice

Dinner
Quick Cutlet Crumble (page 65)
Boiled new potatoes (2 small)
Green salad with Fast French Dressing (page 31)
Wholemeal bread roll spread thinly with polyunsaturated margarine, reduced-fat spread or butter
Fresh fruit
Fruit juice

Snacks
2 slices raisin toast spread thinly with polyunsaturated margarine, reduced-fat spread or butter
2 pieces fresh fruit or 2 glasses fruit juice

DAY 3

Breakfast
Fruit juice
185 g/6 oz fresh fruit salad topped with low-fat yogurt and sprinkled with sultanas
Spring Omelette (page 10)
2 slices wholemeal toast or bread spread thinly with polyunsaturated margarine, reduced-fat spread or butter

Lunch
Rice Pie (page 34)
Green salad with Fast French Dressing (page 31)
2 pieces fresh fruit
Natural mineral water

Dinner
Pork with Red Wine Sauce (page 28)
Steamed new potatoes (2 small)
Generous servings of your favourite steamed vegetables

Wholemeal bread roll spread thinly with polyunsaturated margarine, reduced-fat spread or butter
Fruity Strudel (page 72)
Fruit juice

Snacks
3 Wholemeal Pikelets with Strawberry Spread (page 56)
1 Smashing Smoothie (page 48)
Fruit nectar

DAY 4

Breakfast
Fruit juice
185 g/6 oz fresh fruit salad with low-fat yogurt
Wholegrain breakfast cereal with low-fat milk
2 wholemeal crumpets spread thinly with polyunsaturated margarine, reduced-fat spread or butter, topped with a drizzle of honey

Lunch
Tasty Hawaiian Pockets (page 13)
Fresh fruit
Pineapple Punch (page 50)

Dinner
Mexican Chilli Pasta (page 66)
Green salad with Tangy Cucumber Dressing (page 30)
Wholemeal bread roll spread thinly with polyunsaturated margarine, reduced-fat spread or butter
Fresh fruit
Fruit spritzer (fruit juice and natural mineral water)

Snacks
Speedy Date Slice (page 40)
200 g/6^1/$_2$ oz carton low-fat natural yogurt mixed with dried fruit of your choice
1 piece fresh fruit

DAY 5

Breakfast
Large fruit juice
Fruity Porridge Power (page 12) with low-fat milk and a dollop of low-fat natural yogurt drizzled with honey
Fresh fruit

Lunch
Vegetarian Pan Pizza (page 22)
Green salad with Island Hopping Dressing (page 28)
Wholemeal bread roll spread thinly with polyunsaturated margarine, reduced-fat spread or butter
Get Up and Go Fruit Medley (page 70)
Fruit juice

Dinner
Hot Chicken Curry (page 32)
Steamed vegetables of your choice
Wholemeal bread roll spread thinly with polyunsaturated margarine, reduced-fat spread or butter
Complementary stewed fruit with Apricot Bread Pudding (page 74)
Natural mineral water

Snacks
Pineapple Punch (page 50)
2 slices wholemeal toast spread thinly with polyunsaturated margarine, reduced-fat spread or butter, topped with jam
1 piece fresh fruit

DAY 6

Breakfast
Fruit juice
Mighty Muesli with low-fat milk (page 8)
2 slices wholemeal toast topped with honey mashed banana and cinnamon

Lunch
Multi-layered Bread Loaf (page 16)
Fresh fruit
Fruit juice

Dinner
Vegetable and Lentil Soup (page 62)
Wholemeal bread roll spread thinly with polyunsaturated margarine, reduced-fat spread or butter
Vegetable Pilaf (page 64)
Green salad dressed with lemon vinegar
Summer Pudding (page 74)
Fruit juice

Snacks
2 Ginger 'n' Fruit Cookies (page 38)
Melon Marbles (page 54)
1 Smashing Smoothie (page 48)

DAY 7

Breakfast
Fruit Tango (page 49)
1 cup fruit salad
Wholegrain cereal with low-fat milk
2 Spicy Buckwheat Pancakes (page 10) with Banana Yogurt Topping (page 8)

Lunch
Minestrone Soup (page 24)
Golden Grain Salad (page 14)
Wholegrain bread roll spread thinly with polyunsaturated margarine, reduced-fat spread or butter
200 g/6¹/₂ oz carton low-fat yogurt
Fresh fruit
Fruit juice

Dinner
Chicken Stir-fry (page 61)
Boiled noodles (375 g/12 oz)
Green salad
Creamy Berry Rice (page 72)
Fruit juice

Snacks
2 slices raisin toast spread thinly with polyunsaturated margarine, reduced-fat spread or butter, topped with honey
1 piece fresh fruit

MEAL PLANS EXPLAINED

Each daily menu provides approximately 12,600 kilojoules/3000 Calories: 10,500 kilojoules/2500 Calories from meals, 2100 kilojoules/500 Calories from snacks. The energy (kilojoule/calorie) level is suitable for active males. For females and those less active, smaller servings and reducing or omitting snacks will help to decrease the energy to the appropriate level. Alternatively, increasing foods such as bread, fruit, juice, rice and pasta will increase the energy and carbohydrate in the daily menu.

The proportion of energy from protein, fat and carbohydrate is approximately 20% protein, 20% fat and 60% carbohydrate for Days 1-3. With a view to increasing glycogen stores for a competition on the morning of Day 7 the proportion of carbohydrate was increased on Days 4-7 to 70%, decreasing protein and fat to 15% each.

Serving Sizes

Rice, cooked	1 cup/185 g/6 oz
Fruit juice	1 cup/250 mL/8 fl oz
Rolled oats, cooked	1 cup/250 g/8 oz
Wholegrain cereal	1 cup/30-60 g/1-2 oz

Chicken Stir-fry (page 61)

DIVE INTO A
drink

SMASHING SMOOTHIES

1300 kilojoules/310 Calories per serve (basic recipe) – high carbohydrate; low fat; medium fibre

2 bananas, sliced
2 tablespoons skim milk powder
$^1/_4$ teaspoon ground mixed spice
1 cup/200 g/6$^1/_2$ oz low-fat fruit
salad yogurt
1$^1/_2$ cups/375 mL/12 fl oz skim milk
fresh mint sprigs

Place bananas, milk powder, mixed spice, yogurt and milk in a food processor or blender and process until smooth. Pour into tall chilled glasses and garnish with mint.

Apricot Smoothie: Replace bananas with 250 g/8 oz diced canned apricots and fruit salad yogurt with low-fat apricot yogurt. Omit mixed spice and add 1 teaspoon grated orange rind.

Strawberry Smoothie: Replace bananas with 250 g/8 oz strawberries, and fruit salad yogurt with low-fat strawberry yogurt. Omit mixed spice.

Serves 2

WHAT ABOUT WATER?
Many active people have grown up with the myth that it is detrimental to drink water during exercise.

• Fluid replacement is the most vital of all competition strategies, and failure to replace lost fluids can be detrimental to performance and hazardous to health.

• In most cases water is the best replacement drink.

• Water replacement alone is adequate for short duration or non-endurance events.

• Cold water (5-15°C or refrigerated) is ideal as it empties most rapidly from the stomach.

• In 'ultra' endurance events (longer than three hours) substantial glycogen and salt losses can occur during the competition. Sports (electrolyte replacement) drinks help to replace the carbohydrate and salt along with water.

FRUIT TANGO

450 kilojoules/105 Calories per serve – high carbohydrat; low fat; medium fibre

2 cups/500 mL/16 fl oz orange juice
2 cups/500 mL/16 fl oz apple juice
2 cups/500 mL/16 fl oz pineapple juice
pulp of 4 passion fruit
2 cups/500 mL/16 fl oz sparkling
mineral water
3 tablespoons chopped fresh mint
2 trays ice cubes

Combine orange, apple and pineapple juices and passion fruit pulp in a large punch bowl. Cover and chill until ready to serve. Just prior to serving, add mineral water, mint and ice cubes.

Serves 4

WHAT IS A STANDARD DRINK?
1 standard drink is equal to:
2 x 280 mL/9 fl oz low-
alcohol beer
1 x 280 mL/9 fl oz ordinary
strength beer
1 x 125 mL/4 fl oz table wine
1 x 60 mL/2 fl oz fortified wine
1 x 30 mL/1 fl oz spirits
Recommendations for safe
alcohol consumption:
Women: Up to 1-2 standard
drinks 4-5 times a week.
Men: Up to 3-4 standard
drinks 4-5 times a week.

From left: Egg Flip (page 50), Fruit Tango, Shake It Up (page 50), Pineapple Punch (page 50), Strawberry Smoothie

SHAKE IT UP

1300 kilojoules/310 Calories per serve – high carbohydrate; low fat; low fibre

2 tablespoons skim milk powder
1 scoop vanilla ice cream
1 tablespoon honey
$^1/_2$ teaspoon vanilla essence
1 cup/250 mL/8 fl oz skim milk

Place milk powder, ice cream, honey, vanilla essence and milk in a food processor or blender and process until smooth. Pour into a well-chilled tall glass and serve.

Serves 1

PINEAPPLE PUNCH

1160 kilojoules/275 Calories per serve – high carbohydrate; low fat; low fibre

When exercising thirst is not a good indicator of fluid needs. Once you start to feel thirsty you are already dehydrated so remember to drink small amounts often.

3 tablespoons canned crushed pineapple
1 scoop vanilla ice cream
$^1/_2$ cup/100 g/3$^1/_2$ oz low-fat natural yogurt
$^1/_2$ cup/125 mL/4 fl oz pineapple juice

Place pineapple, ice cream, yogurt and juice in a food processor or blender and process until smooth. Pour into a tall glass and serve.

Serves 1

EGG FLIP

1275 kilojoules/305 Calories per serve – medium carbohydrate; low fat; low fibre

2 tablespoons skim milk powder
1 tablespoon honey
pinch grated nutmeg
1 cup/250 mL/8 fl oz skim milk
1 egg
$^1/_2$ teaspoon vanilla essence

Place milk powder, honey, nutmeg, milk, egg and vanilla essence in a food processor or blender and process until smooth. Pour into a tall glass and sprinkle with extra nutmeg.

Serves 1

Too hot to trot?

Exercise increases the body's heat production. Sweating helps to prevent the body from getting too hot!

To sweat, the body must be well hydrated. If dehydration sets in, body temperature rises and heat stress results. In severe cases permanent physical damage or death can occur. Although athletes sweat more effectively and cope with the heat better than untrained people, they can still experience heat stress.

PREVENTING HEAT STRESS

Regular fluid consumption during exercise helps to replace sweat losses, prevent dehydration and heat stress.

The symptoms of heat stress start slowly. Early warning signs include fatigue, headache, feeling hot, dizzy or nauseous. As the condition worsens, disorientation or incoherence occur and sweating may stop all together. At this stage, most people are too confused to stop themselves and event organisers need to step in. Severe heat stress needs urgent medical attention.

SPORTS DRINKS

Controversy continues over the ideal composition of sports (electrolyte replacement) drinks used during exercise. The major concern is the rate at which they empty from the stomach – the more concentrated the drink, the longer it takes to be emptied from the stomach and absorbed into the blood stream. Delayed emptying is considered to jeopardise hydration and slow-emptying drinks can cause nausea during exercise.

Many new sports drinks, available from pharmacies, contain glucose polymers which empty almost as rapidly as water from the stomach. The glucose helps to delay fatigue and maintain blood sugar levels during exercise. As a general rule, drinks consumed during exercise should not exceed 10 per cent carbohydrate.

REFUELLING

People competing in endurance events extending 2-3 hours need to replace carbohydrates, as well as fluids during competition. Sports drinks combine hydration with refuelling. Carbohydrate-rich foods, in conjunction with sports drinks, also assist carbohydrate and energy replacement.

Those competing in endurance events are advised to consume about 50 grams of carbohydrate per hour. Each athlete needs to experiment to determine which foods work best for them.

FLUID REPLACEMENT

The amount of fluid needed to balance losses depends on the intensity and duration of exercise as well as the environmental conditions. It is not unusual for elite athletes to sweat more than 1 litre per hour.
To replace fluid loss:
- Consume 155-300 mL/5-9½ fl oz of fluid for every 20-30 minutes of strenuous exercise.
- Children and adolescents require 75-200 mL/2½-6½ fl oz of fluid over a similar time frame.
- Ideally, an extra 250-500 mL/ 8-16 fl oz of fluid should be taken 20-30 minutes prior to the event.
- Endurance athletes benefit from increasing their fluid intake 24 hours prior to competition.

9 WAYS TO KEEP COOL
- exercise at cooler times of the day
- gradually acclimatise to weather conditions
- wear comfortable clothing that allows you to sweat freely
- use a sun screen and a hat to protect against the sun's rays
- avoid exercising when you are unwell
- learn to recognise the symptoms of heat stress
- drink cool water regularly
- do not delay drinking – it is too hard to catch up once dehydration sets in
- practise fluid replacement during training

THE SPORTS
canteen

Many sporting clubs and venues have a canteen, but unfortunately the choices of healthy foods can be limited.

Serving healthy food in this environment can help to educate children and parents about the correct diet. As a result, many such places are now switching to health-oriented canteens. A little planning can make them just as popular and profitable as their less healthy predecessors. The following will give you some ideas.

CANTEEN GUIDELINES
The canteen can be important as a practical example of nutrition and health.
• Be involved in the development of your children's, or your own, club's policy on what the canteen should provide for lunches and snacks.
• Follow the Healthy Diet Pyramid plan (available from the Australian Nutrition Foundation and health professionals), which emphasises foods rich in complex carbohydrate, protein, vitamins and minerals and low in fat, sugar and salt.
• Encourage the sale of low-fat foods such as sandwiches and bread rolls with low-fat fillings, and salad and fruit as an alternative to pies, sausage rolls and fried foods.
• Introduce reduced-fat and low-fat milk drinks, yogurt and cheese.
• Have tasting sessions and special promotions – just like the local supermarket does – to find out which foods are the most popular and to promote new ideas.

OTHER CANTEEN FOODS
Throughout this book you will find recipes that are suitable for a sports canteen. Try serving some of the following:
• Multi-layered Bread Loaf (page 16)
• Health Club Sandwiches (page 16)
• Vegetable and Salad Roll-ups (page 18)
• Quick and Easy Quiche (page 26)
• No Fussin' Muffins (page 39)
• Ginger 'n' Fruit Cookies (page 38)
• Wholehearted Rockcakes (page 42)
• Speedy Date Slice (page 40)
• Muesli Slice (page 40)
• Oaty Biscuits (page 42)
• Any of the drinks from the drinks section (pages 48-50)

TROPICAL FREEZERS
282 kilojoules/68 Calories per serve (basic recipe) – high carbohydrate; low fat; low fibre

440 g/14 oz canned crushed pineapple
2 mangoes, flesh chopped
1 banana, sliced
1 tablespoon chopped fresh mint

1 Place pineapple, mangoes, banana and mint in a food processor or blender and process until smooth. Pour mixture into ice cube trays and freeze until firm.

2 Turn fruit freezers out into cups. Eat with fingers.

Strawberry and Watermelon Freezers: Replace pineapple, mangoes and banana with 250 g/8 oz strawberries and 1/4 watermelon, seeds removed and flesh chopped. Omit mint.

Makes 50

Mini Quiches (page 56), Tropical Freezers, Wholemeal Pikelets (page 56)

CRICKET WICKETS

85 kilojoules/20 Calories per serve – low carbohydrate; high fat; negligible fibre

Oven temperature
180°C, 350°F, Gas 4

4 potatoes, cooked and mashed
1 tablespoon skim milk powder
1 tablespoon chopped fresh parsley
pinch cayenne pepper
15 g/¹/₂ oz polyunsaturated margarine, melted
3 tablespoons grated parmesan cheese

1   Combine mashed potatoes with skim milk powder, parsley, cayenne pepper and margarine.

2   Spoon mixture into a piping bag fitted with a large star nozzle, and pipe 7.5 cm/3 in lengths of mixture onto a greased and lined baking tray. Sprinkle with parmesan cheese and bake for 20 minutes or until golden.

Makes 25

MELON MARBLES

180 kilojoules/45 Calories per serve – high carbohydrate; negligible fat; low fibre

¹/₂ rock melon (cantaloupe), seeded
¹/₂ honeydew melon, seeded
¹/₄ watermelon, seeded
2 teaspoons lemon juice
1 teaspoon honey
pulp of 2 passion fruit

Using a melon baller make balls from rock melon (cantaloupe), honeydew melon and watermelon. Combine lemon juice, honey and passion fruit pulp in a bowl. Add melon balls and toss to coat. Thread melon balls, alternately, onto 12 wooden skewers. Chill.

Makes 12

PRICED RIGHT
Use the PRICED principle to treat strains and sprains immediately.
Prevent further injury.
Rest.
Ice reduces pain, swelling and muscle spasm.
Compression. Apply a firm wide bandage over the injured part (the bandage must also extend above and below the injury).
Elevation. Raise the injured part above the level of the heart.
Diagnosis. Go to a qualified professional such as a doctor or physiotherapist.

JAFFLES IN A JIFFY

810 kilojoules/195 Calories per sandwich (ham and pineapple) – medium carbohydrate; medium fat; medium fibre

2 slices wholemeal bread
1 teaspoon 'lite' polyunsaturated margarine

CHOOSE FROM THE FOLLOWING FILLINGS:
1 egg, pan-cooked without fat in a nonstick frying pan
1 tablespoon snipped fresh chives
1 slice reduced-fat-and-salt ham
1 slice reduced-fat cheddar cheese
1 canned pineapple ring, drained
3 tablespoons canned no-added-salt baked beans
1 tablespoon low-fat cottage cheese
2 slices tomato

1   Lightly spread one side of bread with margarine.

2   Place filling of your choice on unspread side of one slice of bread, top with another slice and cook in a jaffle iron or sandwich maker for 2-3 minutes, or until golden.

Makes 1 sandwich

Jaffles in a Jiffy, Melon Marbles, Cricket Wickets

WHOLEMEAL PIKELETS

340 kilojoules/80 Calories per serve – medium carbohydrate; medium fat; low fibre

PIKELETS
³/4 cup/185 mL/6 fl oz skim milk
2 teaspoons polyunsaturated
vegetable oil
1 teaspoon lemon juice
1 egg
2 tablespoons honey
1 cup/155 g/5 oz wholemeal self-
raising flour, sifted with 1 teaspoon
ground cinnamon and husks returned
2 teaspoons polyunsaturated
margarine

STRAWBERRY SPREAD
3 tablespoons reduced-fat ricotta cheese
1 tablespoon low-fat natural yogurt
2 teaspoons honey
250 g/8 oz strawberries, chopped

1 To make pikelets, place skim milk, oil, lemon juice, egg and honey in a food processor or blender and process to combine. Add flour mixture and process until smooth.

2 Melt margarine in a nonstick frying pan. Drop tablespoons of mixture into pan and cook over a medium heat until golden on both sides.

3 To make spread, place ricotta cheese, yogurt and honey in a food processor or blender and process until smooth. Transfer ricotta mixture to a bowl and fold in strawberries. Cover and chill until ready to use.

Serving suggestion: Top pikelets with spread and serve. These pikelets are also delicious served plain.

Makes 12 pikelets

For something different replace strawberries with 2 chopped bananas and add ¹/2 teaspoon grated nutmeg to the spread.

MINI QUICHES

1255 kilojoules/300 Calories per serve (basic recipe) – low carbohydrate; high fat; low fibre

315 g/10 oz prepared wholemeal
shortcrust pastry
1 onion, finely chopped
220 g/7 oz canned no-added-salt
salmon, drained and flaked
2 eggs, lightly beaten
³/4 cup/185 mL/6 fl oz skim milk
¹/4 teaspoon grated nutmeg
2 teaspoons chopped fresh dill
freshly ground black pepper
60 g/2 oz grated reduced-fat
cheddar cheese
1 tablespoon snipped fresh chives

1 Line six 7.5 cm/3 in flan tins with pastry.

2 Cook onion in a nonstick frying pan over a medium heat for 4-5 minutes or until soft. Divide onion and salmon between flans cases. Combine eggs, milk, nutmeg, dill and black pepper to taste. Pour into flans, sprinkle with cheese and chives and bake for 20 minutes or until filling is firm.

Spinach and Ham Quiches: Boil, steam or microwave 100 g/3¹/2 oz chopped spinach until tender. Divide between flan cases. Divide 100 g/3¹/2 oz chopped reduced-fat-and-salt ham and 3 tablespoons finely chopped red pepper between flan cases, then pour over egg mixture, top with cheese and chives and bake for 20 minutes.

Makes 6

Oven temperature
200°C, 400°F, Gas 6

Reduced- or low-fat dairy products are an excellent source of calcium. Some milk products have added calcium and are therefore higher in calcium than regular milk. Reduced- or low-fat dairy foods are useful for people who need to watch their fat or cholesterol intake or for those watching their weight.. These dairy foods are fine for children over the age of 2 years but younger need regular milk to obtain sufficient kilojoules/calories for growth.

Passing the pinch test

There is no such thing as an ideal weight for any height. However, there is a healthy weight range. This is based on a body mass index (BMI) of 20-25. The body mass index is a measure used to assess the appropriateness of body weight for height. It is only appropriate for those over 18 years of age and is not a suitable measurement for children or adolescents, whose weight/height should be assessed using growth charts.

Well trained athletes should be aware that they often fall into the overweight range (BMI 25-30) because of their extra muscle. Therefore BMI is not a useful measure of 'fatness' for athletes or very active people with high muscular development.

Weight scales are the most popular form of determining body weight, however this method is limited as it measures all body components – muscle, bone, fat and water together. As one of the objectives of physical conditioning is to increase muscle and minimise fat, scales do not give you a true indication of fat to muscle portions.

Skinfold measurements are essentially a sophisticated type of 'pinch test', often used to estimate the amount of fat carried on the body. Skinfold measures are most meaningful when done by skilled professionals as a series over a period of time, concentrating on the changes that occur as a result of diet and/or training.

Low body-fat levels are essential for athletes if they are to be competitive in a vast majority of sports. However, fat levels can become an obsession, where even a few millimetres of excess fat seem devastating. Athletes need to understand that body fat will vary from individual to individual and that in some cases 'lower' does not always mean better! In other words, what is best for a team mate may not always be best for you.

MAKE IT OR BREAK IT

Most active people are concerned about how much they weigh. While some sportspeople, such as boxers, rowers, weightlifters and jockeys, have strict weight categories for competition, there is essentially no single ideal weight for any height. Sometimes, competitive athletes can focus too much on a set weight without giving due consideration to how appropriate it is for them.

In some cases, the physique of certain individuals may develop to be unsuitable for the sport or weight category they wish to compete in. This often leads to the use of strict diets, laxatives, saunas, fluid tablets, or perhaps anabolic steroids in an endeavour to change body weight or composition. These methods risk the athlete's health and can result in detrimental physical and psychological effects. If weight cannot be lost sensibly, redirection of effort to a sport better suited to body type will prove less dangerous and more rewarding.

You can work out your BMI by dividing your weight in kilograms by the square of your height in metres.

$$\frac{\text{Weight}}{\text{Height}^2} = \text{BMI}$$

For example if you weigh 70 kg and your height is 1.75 m (i.e. 175 cm)

$$\frac{70}{1.75^2} = 22.86$$

FAMILY FOOD
in a flash

FETTUCCINE VEGETABLE MEDLEY

2355 kilojoules/560 Calories per serve – high carbohydrate; low fat; high fibre

375 g/12 oz spinach fettuccine
375 g/12 oz plain fettuccine

VEGETABLE SAUCE
1 onion, finely chopped
2 cloves garlic, crushed
440 g/14 oz canned no-added-salt
tomatoes, undrained and mashed
6 yellow patty pan squash,
finely sliced
250 g/8 oz asparagus, cut into
5 cm/2 in lengths
155 g/5 oz snow peas (mangetout)
2 zucchini (courgettes), chopped
1 red pepper, chopped
1 tablespoon chopped fresh basil
1/2 cup/125 mL/4 fl oz no-added-salt
tomato purée
30 g/1 oz parmesan cheese shavings

1 Cook pasta in a large saucepan of boiling water following packet directions. Drain and keep warm.

2 To make sauce, place onion, garlic and 1 tablespoon of juice from tomatoes in a saucepan over a medium heat and cook for 3 minutes or until onion is soft. Stir in tomatoes, squash, asparagus, snow peas (mangetout), zucchini (courgettes), red pepper, basil and tomato purée and cook for 4 minutes or until vegetables are tender crisp.

Serving suggestion: Spoon sauce over hot pasta and top with parmesan cheese shavings.

Serves 4

In hot humid weather wear loose-fitting clothes that allow airflow over the skin for efficient cooling. Decrease how hard you exercise, and exercise during the coolest part of the day. In cold conditions wear layers of dry, warm clothing to trap body heat. Cover your head, face and hands to avoid heat loss from these areas and make sure that you warm-up properly.

Tacos to Go (page 60), Fettuccine Vegetable Medley, Gnocchi with Herb Sauce (page 60)

GNOCCHI WITH HERB SAUCE

1015 kilojoules/240 Calories per serve – medium carbohydrate; medium fat; medium fibre

750 g/1½ lb potato gnocchi

FRESH HERB SAUCE
4 tablespoons roughly chopped
fresh parsley
4 tablespoons roughly chopped
fresh coriander
4 tablespoons roughly chopped
fresh basil
2 tablespoons pine nuts
1 tablespoon grated parmesan cheese
1 tablespoon reduced-fat mayonnaise
1 tablespoon vegetable stock
freshly ground black pepper

1 Cook gnocchi in a large saucepan of boiling water following packet directions. Drain and keep warm.

2 To make sauce, place parsley, coriander, basil, pine nuts and parmesan cheese in a food processor or blender and process until combined. Add mayonnaise, stock and black pepper to taste and process until combined.

Serving suggestion: Spoon herb sauce over hot gnocchi and serve immediately. Accompany with steamed green vegetables of your choice or a salad and wholemeal bread rolls.

Serves 4

TACOS TO GO

1480 kilojoules/355 Calories per serve – low carbohydrate; high fat; medium fibre

8 taco shells
60 g/2 oz snow pea (mangetout)
sprouts or watercress
250 g/8 oz cherry tomatoes, sliced
90 g/3 oz grated reduced-fat
cheddar cheese

CHILLI MINCE FILLING
500 g/1 lb lean minced topside
1 large onion, chopped
2 cloves garlic, crushed
1 teaspoon ground cumin
250 g/8 oz canned no-added-salt
tomatoes, drained and mashed
½ cup/125 mL/4 fl oz no-added-salt
tomato purée
1 tablespoon chilli sauce

1 To make filling, heat a nonstick frying pan over a medium heat, add beef, onion and garlic and cook for 5-6 minutes. Stir in cumin, tomatoes, tomato purée and chilli sauce and bring to the boil. Reduce heat and simmer for 10 minutes or until most of the liquid evaporates.

2 Place taco shells on a baking tray and warm in the oven for 5 minutes. Spoon filling into taco shells, then top with snow pea (mangetout) sprouts or watercress, tomato slices and cheese.

Serving suggestion: Tacos make a quick and tasty meal when served with savoury rice and a mixed green salad.

Serves 4

Chicken Stir-fry

CHICKEN STIR-FRY

905 kilojoules/215 Calories per serve – low carbohydrate; low fat; medium fibre

500 g/1 lb boneless chicken breast
fillets, thinly sliced
350 g/11 oz broccoli, broken
into florets
2 small zucchini (courgettes), chopped
1 carrot, sliced
1 red pepper, sliced
2 teaspoons grated fresh ginger
2 tablespoons reduced-salt soy sauce
1 tablespoon honey
1 tablespoon sweet chilli sauce
1 tablespoon hoisin sauce
2 teaspoons cornflour blended with
1 tablespoon water

Serves 4

1   Heat a nonstick frying pan over a medium heat, add chicken and stir-fry for 3-4 minutes or until tender. Remove from pan and set aside.

2   Add broccoli, zucchini (courgettes), carrot and red pepper to pan and stir-fry for 2-3 minutes.

3   Stir in ginger, soy sauce, honey, chilli and hoisin sauces and cornflour mixture and cook, stirring, for 2-3 minutes or until sauce boils and thickens. Return chicken to pan and stir-fry for 2-3 minutes or until heated through.

Serving suggestion: Delicious served on a bed of rice or noodles.

Warming-up gradually gets the heart, lungs, muscles and joints ready for exercise. It should involve 5-10 minutes of general aerobic activity, for example jogging on the spot. Stretch the main muscle groups to be used in the sport and practise skills to be performed during the exercise or game.

VEGETABLE AND LENTIL SOUP

500 kilojoules/120 Calories per serve – high carbohydrate; negligible fat; high fibre

1 onion, finely chopped
6 cups/1.5 litres/2¹/₂ pt vegetable stock
2 carrots, chopped
2 zucchini (courgettes), chopped
1 parsnip, chopped
2 stalks celery, finely chopped
2 tomatoes, peeled, seeded
and chopped
315 g/10 oz red lentils, cooked
1 tablespoon chopped fresh coriander
freshly ground black pepper

1 Place onion and 2 tablespoons stock in a saucepan over a medium heat and cook for 3 minutes or until soft. Stir in carrots, zucchini (courgettes), parsnip, celery and tomatoes, and cook for 2 minutes longer. Add remaining stock, bring to the boil, then reduce heat and simmer for 5-6 minutes.

2 Add lentils, coriander and black pepper to taste and cook 4-5 minutes or until heated through.

Serving suggestion: Accompany with wholemeal bread for a balanced and filling meal.

Serves 4

HURRY CURRY

1360 kilojoules/325 Calories per serve – low carbohydrate; high fat; medium fibre

2 teaspoons polyunsaturated
vegetable oil
500 g/1 lb lamb, trimmed of visible
fat and cut into strips
¹/₂ small cauliflower, broken
into florets
2 onions, cut into eighths
1 red pepper, cubed
2 cloves garlic, crushed
1 tablespoon curry powder
1 teaspoon ground cumin
1 teaspoon ground turmeric
60 g/2 oz frozen peas
3 tablespoons sultanas
1 cup/250 mL/8 fl oz chicken stock
2 teaspoons cornflour blended with
2 tablespoons water
1 cup/200 g/6¹/₂ oz low-fat natural
yogurt
1 teaspoon garam masala

1 Heat oil in a frying pan or wok over a medium heat, add lamb and stir-fry for 3-4 minutes or until meat just changes colour. Remove from pan and set aside.

2 Add cauliflower, onions, red pepper, garlic, curry powder, cumin and turmeric to pan and stir-fry for 5 minutes. Return lamb to pan, stir in peas, sultanas, stock and cornflour mixture and cook, stirring, until curry boils and thickens. Stir in yogurt and garam masala and heat gently without boiling.

Serving suggestion: Accompany curry with steamed rice.

Serves 4

Vegetable Pilaf (page 64), Vegetable and Lentil Soup, Hurry Curry

For some years athletes, particularly endurance athletes, were advised to avoid taking sugar immediately before exercise as it may drop blood sugar levels after exercise begins (theoretically because sugar stimulates the release of the hormone insulin whose job it is to decrease the level of sugar in the blood). Recent research indicates that while sugars can fall, in most cases the effect is transient and does not appear to affect performance. On the other hand, taking sugar immediately before exercise is not thought to benefit performance. Large quantities of concentrated sugar solutions may cause gastric upsets in some individuals.

Sugar on food labels refers to sucrose or table sugar. Other sugars or sweeteners such as fructose (fruit sugar), lactose (milk sugar), glucose, maltose, sorbitol and honey can be added to sweeten foods. Gram for gram, these sweeteners have a similar kilojoule/calorie value to sugar. Labels on products can legally state 'no added sugar' providing there is no sucrose. If you are watching your sugar or kilojoule/calorie intake, look on the label for sugars 'incognito'. By contrast, saccharine, cyclamate and Nutrasweet have negligible kilojoules/calories.

VEGETABLE PILAF

950 kilojoules/225 Calories per serve – high carbohydrate; low fat; high fibre

2 teaspoons polyunsaturated
vegetable oil
2 red onions, sliced
1 clove garlic, crushed
315 g/10 oz broccoli, cut into florets
315 g/10 oz cauliflower, cut
into florets
250 g/8 oz patty pan squash, sliced
185 g/6 oz button mushrooms, cut
into quarters
1 red pepper, chopped
2 cups/440 g/14 oz brown rice,
cooked

1   Heat oil in a frying pan over a
medium heat, add onions and garlic and
cook for 3 minutes or until onion is
soft. Add broccoli, cauliflower, squash,
mushrooms and red pepper and cook
for 4-5 minutes or until vegetables are
tender crisp.

2   Stir in rice and cook for 5 minutes
longer or until rice is heated through.

Serving suggestion: Accompany with
mixed bean and tossed green salads.

Serves 4

TAGLIATELLE WITH TUNA

1575 kilojoules/375 Calories per serve – medium carbohydrate; low fat; medium fibre

375 g/12 oz dried wholemeal
tagliatelle or spaghetti

TUNA SAUCE
1 onion, finely chopped
1 clove garlic, crushed
440 g/14 oz canned no-added-salt
tomatoes, undrained and mashed
2 zucchini (courgettes), sliced
1 tablespoon no-added-salt tomato
paste (purée)
1 tablespoon dry red wine
440 g/14 oz canned tuna in spring
water, drained and flaked
1 tablespoon shredded fresh basil
freshly ground black pepper

1   Cook pasta in a large saucepan of
boiling water following packet directions.
Drain and keep warm.

2   To make sauce, heat a nonstick
frying pan over a medium heat, add
onion, garlic and 1 tablespoon of juice
from tomatoes and cook for 4-5 minutes
or until onion is soft. Stir in tomatoes,
zucchini (courgettes), tomato paste
(purée) and wine and cook, stirring,
over a low heat for 5 minutes.

3   Add tuna, basil and black pepper
to taste and cook gently until heated
through.

Serving suggestion: Place pasta on
serving plates, spoon sauce over and
garnish with basil. Serve with a mixed
lettuce and herb salad and crusty bread.

Serves 4

Cooling-down allows the
body's systems to gradually
slow down. To cool down do
the same activities as you
did for warming-up (see hint
on page 61) but in the
reverse order.

To make Tuna Sauce in the
microwave, place onion
and garlic in a microwavable
dish and cook on HIGH
(100%) for 2 minutes. Stir
in zucchini (courgettes),
tomatoes, tomato paste
(purée) and wine and
cook on HIGH (100%) for
3-4 minutes longer. Add
tuna, basil and black
pepper to taste and
cook on HIGH (100%) for
3-4 minutes longer.

Quick Cutlet Crumble, Tagliatelle with Tuna

QUICK CUTLET CRUMBLE

1360 kilojoules/325 Calories per serve – low carbohydrate; medium fat; medium fibre

4 x 200 g/6¹/₂ oz white fish cutlets
2 tablespoons lime juice

HERB TOPPING
2 cups/125 g/4 oz wholemeal
breadcrumbs, made from stale bread
¹/₂ cup/45 g/1¹/₂ oz instant rolled oats
2 tablespoons chopped fresh coriander
2 tablespoons snipped fresh chives
1 tablespoon vinegar
2 teaspoons olive oil
freshly ground black pepper

1 To make topping, place breadcrumbs, rolled oats, coriander, chives, vinegar, oil and black pepper to taste in a bowl and mix to combine. Set aside.

2 Brush fish cutlets with lime juice and cook under a preheated hot grill for 5 minutes on one side.

3 Turn fish over and cover each cutlet with some of the topping. Grill for 5 minutes longer or until cooked through and topping is golden.

Serving suggestion: Garnish with lemon and accompany with new potatoes and a green salad.

Serves 4

Stretch each muscle at least twice before exercise and once after exercise. Do not bounce or stretch rapidly. Do not hold your breath while stretching. Hold each stretch for 30-60 seconds.

HONEY BEEF

1180 kilojoules/280 Calories per serve – low carbohydrate; high fat; low fibre

1 tablespoon polyunsaturated
vegetable oil
500 g/1 lb lean rump steak, cut into
thin strips
1 parsnip, cut into thin strips
1 red pepper, cut into thin strips
4 spinach leaves, shredded
3 spring onions, cut diagonally into
2.5 cm/1 in lengths
1 clove garlic, crushed
2 teaspoons grated fresh ginger
$^1/_3$ cup/90 mL/3 fl oz reduced-salt
soy sauce
2 teaspoons cornflour blended with
2 tablespoons dry sherry
2 teaspoons honey

1 Heat 2 teaspoons oil in a frying pan or wok over a medium heat, add beef, parsnip, red pepper, spinach and spring onions and stir-fry for 2-3 minutes or until meat changes colour. Remove mixture from pan and set aside.

2 Add remaining oil to pan and heat. Add garlic and ginger and stir-fry for 1-2 minutes, then return beef mixture to the pan. Combine soy sauce, cornflour mixture and honey, stir into pan and cook, stirring, for 1-2 minutes or until heated through. Serve immediately.

Serves 4

MEXICAN CHILLI PASTA

2540 kilojoules/605 Calories per serve – high carbohydrate; low fat; high fibre

750 g/1$^1/_2$ lb tomato fettuccine

MEXICAN CHILLI SAUCE
2 onions, chopped
1 clove garlic, crushed
2 fresh red chillies, finely chopped
1 tablespoon water
440 g/14 oz canned red kidney beans,
drained
440 mL/14 fl oz canned no-added-salt
tomato purée

1 Cook fettuccine in boiling water in a large saucepan following packet directions. Drain and keep warm.

2 To make sauce, place onions, garlic, chillies and water in saucepan over a medium heat and cook for 3-4 minutes or until onion is soft. Stir in red kidney beans and tomato purée and bring to the boil. Reduce heat and simmer for 4-5 minutes or until sauce thickens.

Serving suggestion: Spoon sauce over pasta and serve with a tossed green salad.

Serves 4

Mexican Chilli Pasta, Honey Beef

Fat Finder

Low-fat diets assist active people to maintain their lean physique. Most Western diets contain too much fat. Since fats have more kilojoules (calories) than any other nutrient, excessive intake may lead to obesity. Fat should ideally provide less than 30 per cent of daily energy. Athletes range from being too blase to obsessive about fat intake; neither extreme is good.

TYPES OF FAT

Triglycerides and cholesterol are the two main groups of fat in our diet. Intake of both needs to be kept to a minimum.
Cholesterol: This is found in foods such as liver, kidney, egg yolk, butter and cheese. Excessive cholesterol intake has been linked with coronary heart disease, but it is now regarded to be less important than the excessive intake of saturated fat.

There are three main types of triglycerides:
Saturated: These include butter, lard, cheese, fat on meat, coconut and whole milk. It should be noted an excess of saturated fat is linked with elevated blood cholesterol and coronary heart disease. Replacing this fat with either mono-unsaturated or polyunsaturated fat is recommended.
Mono-unsaturated: These include olive, peanut or canola oil and avocado.
Polyunsaturated: These include sunflower, safflower, fish, fish oils and polyunsaturated margarine.

In practical terms it is easy to cut down on visible fat, such as spreads, the fat on meat or skin on chicken, salad dressings or that extra dollop of cream. However, to successfully cut fat we need to be aware of the hidden fats in food. The list opposite will assist you in recognising some of these sources.

Travellers' tales

As the food supplied at sports venues is not necessarily designed to be healthy, competitors need to be prepared.

LOCAL EVENTS

• Take suitable foods with you.
• Packaged foods such as breads, cereals, juices or fruits (fresh, dried or canned) travel well.
• Commercially available sports drinks are a convenient snack and are a great back up.
• Take plain water to unfamiliar venues. Many sporting venues do not provide bubblers or water coolers for competitors.
• For large teams, special meals at restaurants and hotels can be organised. The team will not only eat better but, in general, more quickly.
• When competitors are away for several days consider the cooking facilities, food or menu that is available. Thinking ahead saves time and ensures competitors eat well.
• If staying at a hotel, stock the refrigerator with essentials such as cereals, juices, fruits, bread and milk.

OVERSEAS

The suggestions for competing at local events, with a few moderations, can be applied to overseas travel.
• Write out an itinerary of the countries to be visited and do a little research as to the types of foods likely to be available, safety of the water supply in the area, cost of food (so it can be included in your travel budget), and customs regulations regarding taking special sports drinks with you.
• The large variety and amount of food offered in athlete villages can be a temptation for many people. Aim to keep to your usual routine.

8 WAYS TO PREVENT JETLAG
• do some light exercise before the flight
• request a seat in the non-smoking section
• keep to 'home' time during the flight
• adjust to the new time schedule when you arrive
• drink liberal amounts of water
• stand up and stretch your legs on long flights
• avoid excess coffee, tea, cola drinks or alcohol
• eat moderately

EATING IN UNFAMILIAR PLACES

Use the following checklist to help prevent illness:
• Use boiled, sterilised or bottled water. If the water supply is unsafe to drink, remember to avoid ice also.
• If bottled water is not available, canned or bottled soft drinks are preferable to the local water supply.
• If the water supply is unsafe, avoid anything raw which may be washed in water.
• Avoid all unpasteurised dairy products. If in doubt about pasteurisation, use long-life or powdered milk (made with sterile water).
• Watch how the food is handled. If you are in doubt about the hygiene, behind the scenes is likely to be worse! Eat at another venue.

TRAVELLERS' DIARRHOEA

One of the dangers of overseas travel is gastroenteritis, or so-called travellers' diarrhoea, symptoms for which include loose/frequent bowel motions, stomach cramps, nausea, vomiting and possibly fever. It has been estimated that travellers' diarrhoea affects between 30-60 per cent of athletes who travel overseas. Aside from the discomfort, the physical and psychological effects can be devastating and may prevent athletes from competing at all. Preventing the problem revolves around choosing food and fluids from hygienic outlets. The local water supply may also need to be avoided.

Pumping up the iron

Iron is best known for its presence in haemoglobin, a component of the red blood cells. Haemoglobin transports oxygen to (and carbon dioxide away from) the body's tissues and muscles. If insufficient iron is obtained from food, iron deficiency anaemia is likely to occur.

IRON

Iron in the diet is found in two forms:
Haem iron is well absorbed by the body. It is found in 'flesh' foods such as meat, poultry, and seafood. Liver and kidney are the richest sources.
Non-haem iron is found in plant foods and includes breakfast cereals, rice, pasta, bread, vegetables, dried peas and beans. It is less well absorbed by the body.

IRON DEFICIENCY ANAEMIA

People in heavy training appear to be at increased risk of developing iron-deficiency anaemia. Some of the reasons to explain this are:
Increased iron loss: Blood loss from injuries and that resulting from friction on internal organs and red blood cells (due to jarring exercises) can increase iron loss. Iron is also lost in sweat.
Decreased intake: People following 'fad' or strict weight-reducing diets often decrease their intake of iron-rich sources, such as red meat.
Decreased absorption: People in heavy training may have decreased iron absorption. Further research is required to confirm and investigate the reasons for this.

Diagnosis of anaemia: Doctors need to take a blood test to determine if a person is anaemic. This test can measure the iron in blood cells (haemoglobin) as well as the body's stores of iron (ferritin). Fatigue and decreased athletic performance have been associated with the early stages of anaemia (low ferritin). Symptoms at later stages are more severe and include fatigue, dizziness and possibly shortness of breath. An adequate iron intake helps to prevent anaemia.

RECOMMENDED IRON INTAKE

Children	6-8 mg/day
Adolescents	10-13 mg/day
Adults	
Male	7 mg/day
Female	12-16 mg/day
While pregnant	22-36 mg/day

6 WAYS TO PUMP UP IRON
- include haem iron (meat, fish, poultry) in your daily diet
- eat red meat 3-4 times a week
- liver and kidney are the richest sources of haem iron
- if you are a vegetarian your iron will come from non-haem sources (legumes, rice, pasta, vegetables, etc.)
- enhance absorption of non-haem iron by regularly including vitamin C rich foods (e.g. citrus fruits) with meals
- avoid excessive consumption of caffeine (tea, coffee and cola drinks) and unprocessed bran which can reduce absorption of non-haem iron

GOOD FOOD SOURCES OF IRON

FOOD	SERVE SIZE	IRON (mg)
Beef kidney (simmered)	1 cup/155 g/5 oz, diced	11.4
Beef liver (simmered)	1 cup/140 g/4^1/2 oz, diced	9.1
Lean rump steak (grilled)	1 steak (185 g/6 oz)	6.8
Veal leg steak (lean, baked)	2 slices (90 g/3 oz)	1.6
Pork leg (lean, baked)	2 slices (90 g/3 oz)	1.6
Lamb chump chop (lean, grilled)	1 chop (60 g/2 oz)	2.0
Chicken breast (skin removed)	half breast (75 g/2^1/2 oz)	0.5
Red salmon	100 g/3^1/2 oz	1.2
Tuna (in oil)	100 g/3^1/2 oz	0.6
Oysters (raw)	12 oysters	2.3
Red kidney beans	1 cup/170 g/5^1/2 oz, boiled	3.8
Spinach	1 cup/140 g/4^1/2 oz, cooked	4.4
Rolled oats	1 cup/250 g/8 oz, cooked	1.8
Wholemeal bread	1 slice (30 g/1 oz)	0.7

Reprinted with permission. Source: Commonwealth Department of Community Services and Health 1989, NUTTAB Version 89. Food Industry Data.

TIME FOR A
treat

❦

STRAWBERRY CHEESECAKE
925 kilojoules/220 Calories per serve – low carbohydrate; medium fat; medium fibre

100 g/3¹/₂ oz wheatmeal biscuit crumbs
30 g/1 oz polyunsaturated margarine, melted
2 teaspoons water

STRAWBERRY FILLING
3 tablespoons raspberry jelly crystals
1 tablespoon gelatine
1 cup/250 mL/8 fl oz boiling water
²/₃ cup/140 g/4¹/₂ oz low-fat natural yogurt
1 cup/250 g/8 oz low-fat cottage cheese
pulp of 3 passion fruit
250 g/8 oz strawberries, hulled and halved

1 Place biscuit crumbs, margarine and water in a bowl and mix to combine. Press mixture over base of a lightly greased 20 cm/8 in springform tin and refrigerate until firm.

2 Place jelly crystals and gelatine in a bowl, pour over water and mix to dissolve. Cool to room temperature. Place yogurt and cottage cheese in a food processor or blender and process until smooth. Add jelly mixture and process until combined. Stir in passion fruit pulp. Pour mixture in tin and refrigerate until almost set. Arrange strawberries over top of cheesecake and chill until set.

Serves 6

❦

GET UP AND GO FRUIT MEDLEY
1540 kilojoules/365 Calories per serve – high carbohydrate; low fat; high fibre

250 g/8 oz dried fruit salad mix
90 g/3 oz dried fruit medley
1 cup/250 mL/8 fl oz apricot nectar or orange juice
3 tablespoons lemon juice
3 tablespoons brandy
2 teaspoons honey, warmed
1 apple, chopped
250 g/8 oz strawberries
250 g/8 oz grapes or melon pieces
1 kiwifruit, sliced
4 tablespoons low-fat natural yogurt

Place fruit salad mix, fruit medley, apricot nectar or orange juice, lemon juice, brandy and honey in a saucepan over a medium heat. Bring to the boil, then reduce heat and simmer for 10 minutes. Add apple, strawberries, grapes or melon and kiwifruit and mix to combine. Serve hot or chilled with low-fat yogurt.

Serves 4

Honey and sugar (brown, white or raw) are both simple carbohydrates that provide energy (kilojoules/calories), yet insignificant amounts of vitamins or minerals. There is no health benefit in substituting honey, brown or raw sugar for white sugar.

Strawberry Cheesecake, Creamy Berry Rice (page 72), Get Up and Go Fruit Medley

CREAMY BERRY RICE

1090 kilojoules/260 Calories per serve – high carbohydrate; low fat; medium fibre

½ cup/100 g/3½ oz short grain rice
125 g/4 oz blueberries
125 g/4 oz raspberries
4 tablespoons low-fat natural yogurt
3 tablespoons low-fat berry-flavoured yogurt
¾ cup/185 mL/6 fl oz evaporated skim milk
1 tablespoon honey
½ teaspoon ground mixed spice

1 Cook rice in boiling water in a large saucepan for 10-12 minutes or until tender. Drain and rinse under cold running water.

2 Place rice, blueberries, raspberries, natural and berry yogurts, evaporated milk, honey and mixed spice in a bowl and mix to combine. Spoon into individual serving dishes and chill.

Variation: You might like to use chopped, drained, canned fruits such as peaches, pears or apricots in place of the berries, and a complementary fruit-flavoured yogurt in place of the berry yogurt.

Serves 4

Fresh fruit and vegetables subjected to the environment after picking lose vitamins. The amount lost depends on handling and how long before they are consumed. Snap-frozen vegetables escape excessive environmental exposure and often have a higher content of vitamins than those bought from the greengrocer. Although vitamins are inevitably lost with food handling and processing, a varied and well balanced diet will provide plenty of vitamins.

FRUITY STRUDEL

1350 kilojoules/320 Calories per serve – high carbohydrate; low fat; medium fibre

5 sheets filo pastry
15 g/½ oz polyunsaturated margarine, melted
2 teaspoons sugar

APPLE AND PEAR FILLING
1 apple, chopped
2 pears, chopped
125 g/4 oz dried mixed fruit
1 cup/60 g/2 oz wholemeal breadcrumbs, made from stale bread
3 tablespoons caster sugar
½ teaspoon ground cinnamon
1 teaspoon grated lemon rind
2 tablespoons orange juice

1 To make filling, place apple, pears, dried fruit, breadcrumbs, caster sugar, cinnamon, lemon rind and orange juice in saucepan and bring to the boil. Reduce heat, cover and simmer for 10 minutes or until mixture thickens. Cool.

2 Layer pastry sheets, brushing every second layer with margarine. Spoon filling diagonally across pastry sheets, then roll up, turning in sides as you roll. Place on a lightly greased baking tray, brush top with a little margarine and sprinkle with sugar. Bake for 10-15 minutes or until golden.

Serves 4

Oven temperature
200°C, 400°F, Gas 6

ORANGE CREME CARAMELS

940 kilojoules/225 Calories per serve – high carbohydrate; low fat; low fibre

CARAMEL
¹/₂ cup/125 g/4 oz sugar
¹/₂ cup/125 mL/4 fl oz water

ORANGE CUSTARD
¹/₂ cup/30 g/2 oz skim milk powder, sifted
3 tablespoons caster sugar
4 eggs, lightly beaten
1 teaspoon vanilla essence
2 cups/500 mL/16 fl oz skim milk, scalded
1 tablespoon grated orange rind

1   To make Caramel, place sugar and water in a heavy-based saucepan over a low heat and cook, stirring constantly, until sugar dissolves. Bring to the boil and boil, without stirring, until mixture turns a light golden colour. Divide mixture between six lightly greased ¹/₂ cup/125 mL/4 fl oz capacity ramekins.

2   To make custard, place milk powder, sugar, eggs and vanilla essence in a bowl and beat until sugar dissolves. Whisk in milk and orange rind, then pour into ramekins.

3   Place ramekins in a baking dish with enough boiling water to come halfway up sides of ramekins and bake for 20 minutes or until a knife inserted into the centre comes out clean.

4   Remove ramekins from baking dish and set aside to cool. Chill.

Serving suggestion: Invert chilled desserts onto serving plates and accompany with canned or stewed apricots.

Serves 6

Oven temperature
180°C, 350°F, Gas 4

To scald milk, rinse a small, heavy-based saucepan with cold water, add milk and bring almost to the boil over a low heat, stirring occasionally. Scalding helps prevent curdling during cooking.

Orange Crème Caramels

APRICOT BREAD PUDDING

1605 kilojoules/385 Calories per serve – medium carbohydrate; low fat; high fibre

Oven temperature
180°C, 350°F, Gas 4

Yolk-free egg mix is a low cholesterol mix and is available as a frozen product from supermarkets. It is made from egg whites, polyunsaturated vegetable oil and skim milk and can be used in cooking in place of whole eggs. One sachet (100 g/3^1/$_2$ oz) is the equivalent of two whole eggs.

10 slices wholemeal bread, crusts removed
75 g/2^1/$_2$ oz dried apricots, chopped
200 g/6^1/$_2$ oz yolk-free egg mix, thawed
1 cup/250 mL/8 fl oz evaporated skim milk
2 cups/500 mL/16 fl oz skim milk
2 tablespoons honey
^{1}/$_2$ teaspoon ground cinnamon

1   Cut each slice of bread in half diagonally. Arrange one-third of the bread triangles in a lightly greased 20 cm/8 in soufflé dish. Sprinkle with half the apricots and layer with another one-third of the bread triangles. Top with remaining apricots and bread, placing 6 triangles around the outside of the dish and cover pudding with remaining slices.

2   Place egg mix, evaporated and skim milks and honey in a bowl and whisk to combine. Pour over bread then sprinkle with cinnamon.

3   Place soufflé dish in a baking dish with enough boiling water to come halfway up the sides of the dish and bake for 40 minutes or until a knife inserted into the centre comes out clean.

Serves 4

SUMMER PUDDING

1290 kilojoules/310 Calories per serve – high carbohydrate; low fat; high fibre

250 g/8 oz blueberries
^{1}/$_4$ cup/45 g/1^1/$_2$ oz brown sugar
^{1}/$_3$ cup/90 mL/3 fl oz blackcurrant juice
440 g/14 oz canned stoneless cherries, drained
250 g/8 oz strawberries, hulled
200 g/6^1/$_2$ oz raspberries
10 slices wholemeal bread, crusts removed

1   Place blueberries, brown sugar and blackcurrant juice in saucepan over a low heat and cook for 5-10 minutes or until berries are tender. Stir in cherries, strawberries and raspberries. Cool.

2   Line a 4 cup/1 litre/1^3/$_4$ pt pudding basin with bread. Spoon half the cooled fruit mixture into basin and top with a layer of bread. Add remaining fruit and finish with a layer of bread. Pour over any remaining liquid.

3   Place a saucer small enough to fit inside the basin on top of pudding and weigh it down with a 500 g/1 lb weight (a can of fruit or bowl of water is ideal). Refrigerate overnight.

Serving suggestion: Turn onto a serving plate and cut into wedges.

Serves 4

The fruit mixture can be cooked in the microwave. Place blueberries, brown sugar and blackcurrant juice in a microwavable dish and cook on HIGH (100%) for 3-4 minutes. Complete as directed in the recipe.

*Fruity Strudel (page 72),
Apricot Bread Pudding*

MELON AND YOGURT CUPS

605 kilojoules/155 Calories per serve – high carbohydrate; low fat; medium fibre

2 small rock melons (cantaloupes),
    halved and seeds removed
2 nectarines, stones removed
    and sliced
155 g/5 oz strawberries, sliced
155 g/5 oz black grapes

YOGURT DRESSING
1 kiwifruit, roughly chopped
³/₄ cup/155 g/5 oz low-fat
    natural yogurt
1 tablespoon honey

1 To make dressing, place kiwifruit,
yogurt and honey in a bowl and mix
to combine.

2 Place melon halves on individual
serving plates. Fill with nectarines,
strawberries and grapes. Spoon over
dressing and chill.

Serves 4

Try this tempting fruit
combination for breakfast.

PEACHY CRUNCHY CRUMBLE

1450 kilojoules/345 Calories per serve – medium carbohydrate; medium fat; high fibre

Oven temperature
180°C, 350°F, Gas 4

2 x 440 g/14 oz canned peach halves,
drained and liquid reserved
pulp of 2 passion fruit
³/₄ cup/90 g/3 oz untoasted muesli
2 tablespoons flour
1 tablespoon brown sugar
30 g/1 oz polyunsaturated margarine
4 tablespoons chopped walnuts
1 teaspoon ground cinnamon

1   Pour reserved peach liquid into a shallow ovenproof dish. Then arrange peach halves cavity side up in dish. Spoon a little passion fruit pulp into each cavity.

2   Combine muesli, flour and sugar, then rub in margarine and stir in walnuts and cinnamon. Sprinkle mixture over peaches and bake for 20 minutes.

Serving suggestion: Serve with low-fat natural or fruit-flavoured yogurt.

Serves 4

This dessert can also be made using canned apricot or pear halves.

CREPE ESCAPES

1555 kilojoules/370 Calories per serve – low carbohydrate; medium fat; medium fibre

1 cup/125 g/4 oz flour
2 eggs, lightly beaten
1 cup/250 mL/8 fl oz skim milk

RICOTTA AND PINEAPPLE
FILLING
200 g/6¹/₂ oz reduced-fat ricotta
cheese
3 tablespoons flaked almonds, toasted
1 tablespoon honey
1 mango, thinly sliced
220 g/7 oz canned pineapple pieces,
drained
shredded coconut, toasted

The crêpes can be made ahead of time, simply cook them and allow to cool. Then stack crêpes, interleaved with plastic food wrap, place in a freezer bag and freeze for up to 3 months. Reheat frozen crêpes in the microwave for 20 seconds per crêpe, or until just warm. Fill and serve.

1   Sift flour in a bowl. Combine eggs and milk and stir in flour a little at a time until mixture is smooth. Stand for 30 minutes.

2   Heat a nonstick frying pan over a medium heat, pour in 3 tablespoons of mixture and cook until golden on both sides. Remove from pan and keep warm. Repeat with remaining mixture.

3   To make filling, place ricotta cheese, almonds and honey in a bowl and mix to combine. Place spoonfuls of ricotta mixture on one half of each crêpe. Top with mango and pineapple, then fold crêpes into triangles. Sprinkle with shredded coconut and serve immediately.

Variation: Any fruit can be used in place of the mango and pineapple. You might like to use fresh berries, canned or fresh apricots, peaches or pears.

Serves 4

Summer Pudding (page 74), Peachy Crunchy Crumble, Crêpe Escapes

Sports report

Alcohol, smoking, caffeine, anabolic steriods – how do these affect sportspeople? This section answers many of the questions and the myths.

Alcohol: This has long been associated with the 'sporting image'. Many people believe that alcohol does no harm as long as they 'sweat it off'. Excessive alcohol consumption is dangerous, no matter how fit you are or how hard you train. Hard exercise with a hangover is dangerous and is not recommended – it does not sober you up faster! Alcohol slows reaction time, impairs coordination and concentration, and is a poor source of carbohydrate. The dehydrating properties adversely affect temperature regulation, increasing the risk of heat stress during exercise, and delaying rehydration after exercise.

For the weight-conscious, it is a source of kilojoules (calories) that has little nutritional value. Excessive alcohol consumption is also known to deplete the body of certain vitamins and minerals, especially thiamin (vitamin B1), folic acid, zinc, magnesium and potassium. The following guidelines will assist you to drink safely:
• Keep to the recommended 'safe' levels (see page 49). Do not save up a week's alcohol intake for one night! Minimal intake is recommended for people in heavy training.
• Abstain from alcohol 24-48 hours before sports events.
• After competition, replace sweat losses with water or carbohydrate-rich drinks followed by a carbohydrate-rich meal. Avoid drinking alcohol immediately after exercise or on an empty stomach.
• Avoid heavy exercise after large amounts of alcohol.

Smoking: Cigarette smoking may deplete the body's vitamin C levels and increases the risk of developing various diseases such as:
• cancers of the lung, mouth and upper respiratory tract;
• bronchitis;
• emphysema;
• high blood pressure; and
• vascular disease.
In the Western world, smoking is the greatest preventable cause of disease. All of us experience smoking to some extent, because of our exposure to others who smoke – referred to as passive smoking.

Smoking adversely affects athletic performance by hampering the movement of air in and out of the lungs and limiting the transport of oxygen around the body. Exercise does not prevent the adverse effects of smoking. In the interests of good health and peak performance, you should stop smoking now.

Marijuana and hashish: These substances offer no benefit to athletic performance. The immediate effects of these drugs include elevated heart rate and blood pressure, impairment of coordination, concentration and decreased sensation. Loss of short-term memory, anxiety, confusion, and inflammation of the delicate lung tissues may also occur. Temperature regulation is also impaired.

DRUGS AND SPORT

In the pursuit of speed, skill, endurance and power some athletes look to drugs as a means of enhancing performance. The first reported use of drugs for sport dates back to the 3rd century BC. In this case, a hallucinogenic extract from a particular variety of mushrooms was used to enhance performance. Over the years, drug use has become more sophisticated – but it is no less dangerous!

Drug testing for national and international competitions is not standard practice to protect the health of athletes and to keep sport as a competition of natural abilities. Athletes found to have been using drugs are subject to disqualification and perhaps permanent dismissal from competition. A wide range of drugs are banned from competitions, and some of them are included in 'over-the-counter' preparations. Even a small quantity is sufficient to give a positive drug test. Athletes need to be aware of the health risks and legal aspects of drug taking. They should always seek medical advice prior to taking any medication before a competition.

BANNED DRUGS
The following is a list of some of the banned drugs:
Adrenaline and ephedrine*; Cocaine; Amphetamines*; Nicotine; Caffeine*; Sympathomimetic amines*; Analgesics (pain killers); Beta blockers; Diuretics; Anabolic steroids; Growth hormone.
*These can be in products and medications bought over the counter.

Caffeine: Used by athletes to stimulate the central nervous system and enhance arousal. Also used by endurance athletes to increase free fatty acid release and delay fatigue. Whilst the ability of caffeine to stimulate the central nervous system is well accepted, its ability to delay fatigue is still controversial. Detrimental effects include insomnia, gastric irritation, and mild increase in blood pressure and body temperature. The diuretic properties may be detrimental to hydration and temperature regulation during exercise. Excessive caffeine may adversely affect iron and calcium balance. Abuse may lead to disqualification.

Anabolic steroids: These have been used by athletes to increase muscle bulk and strength. Although the efficacy of steroids, especially with respect to their ability to increase strength has been questioned, they do appear to enhance athletic performance – at least in some athletes. **Steroids, however, have many detrimental side effects** which include liver toxicity and increased risk of liver cancer and heart disease, acne, fluid retention, aggression, and altered libido. In men, baldness and decreased sperm production can occur. In women, menstruation may cease, physical features may become more masculine, and there is usually increased body hair. Steroids may stunt the growth of children.

Every sportsperson should be aware that their use for sport is both illegal and dangerous.

SUPPLEMENTS

Vitamins: The need for vitamin supplements in athletes is a controversial issue. Some sportspeople would have us believe that they are beneficial. The vast majority of research shows that, providing a well-balanced diet is eaten, vitamin supplements do not enhance athletic performance. Some people rely on vitamins to make up for a poor diet. Supplements do nothing to improve the carbohydrate content or reduce the fat content of the diet and it is usually these factors rather than a lack of vitamins that need most attention. Large doses of vitamins have the potential to be toxic and possibly interfere with the normal absorption of other nutrients in the diet. Active people following well-balanced diets should not require vitamin supplements. For those who feel insecure without supplements, a low-dose multivitamin is the best choice. It is important that these supplements never be regarded as a food substitute. One exception to this is when athletes are travelling for substantial periods. Under these circumstances, a multivitamin supplement may help to support intake which can be less varied or balanced than their usual diet.

Minerals: Calcium and iron supplements may sometimes be required by athletes in heavy training. For further information consult a health professional.

Be healthy, be slim

Anorexia nervosa is characterised by:
- an intense desire to be slim
- dramatic weight loss due to self starvation
- in some cases excessive exercise
- normal amounts of food appear excessive
- every kilojoule (calorie) consumed is often counted
- menstruation may become irregular or stop all together

A major proportion of the weight-loss diets promoted to the public are based on 'fads' and have no scientific basis. The following checklist will help you to judge whether your diet is a sensible one.

DIETERS' CHECKLIST

- The diet should include a variety of foods like bread and cereals, fruits and vegetables, lean meat and alternatives (eggs, poultry, seafood and legumes), dairy foods and limited amounts of fats and oils. Some food from each food group needs to be included daily.
- The diet needs to include regular meals that will fit into your lifestyle.
- The energy level should not be less than 4200 kilojoules (1000 Calories) per day. Active people rarely need diets less than 6300 kilojoules (1500 Calories) per day.
- The diet should allow for a gradual weight loss of 0.5-1 kg per week. Rapid weight reduction increases the loss of water and muscle. Weight loss in overweight children or adolescents needs to be managed carefully as growth may be compromised if losses are rapid. Weight maintenance or, at most, gradual weight loss is recommended. In this way they can 'grow out' of their excess weight.
- The diet should use regular foods and not include special supplements.

EATING DISORDERS

Looking slim is fashionable in our society and many people exercise specifically to achieve or maintain a slim body. For some, such as ballet dancers, gymnasts and figure skaters, slimness is also an aesthetic requirement. Even at the non-elite level there is often intense pressure to maintain a slim body. Some people participating in these sports have a metabolism and body type which lends itself to slimness. They seemingly have little difficulty in maintaining the right weight or shape. Others fight a constant battle to achieve what is sometimes an unrealistic weight for them.

Disordered eating, such as anorexia nervosa or bulimia, is closely associated with social pressures or personal desires to be slim. It is more common in young women than men.

While dieting for cosmetic or competitive reasons is a common feature of disordered eating, there may also be other underlying psychological problems. People with an eating disorder usually need to seek outside counselling – nutritional, psychological or a combination of both. Early diagnosis and treatment is often difficult as those affected generally deny they have the condition.

Athletes, coaches and parents need to be realistic about how appropriate a particular weight or body fat goal is and give due consideration to the physical and psychological dangers associated with the pressure of imposing too inflexible and unrealistic goals.

Bulimia is characterised by:
- periods of starvation as in anorexia
- but these are broken by binges where large quantities of food are consumed
- in some cases, self-induced vomiting, laxatives or diuretics are used
- bulimics are not typically underweight, they may be overweight or normal weight

Index